Hollywood GETS *Married*

For Tula —
See you at the
movies!
Best, Sandy Schwier

Hollywood GETS Married

SANDY SCHREIER

CLARKSON POTTER / PUBLISHERS
NEW YORK

Photo credits: Page 10: (left) Associated Press, (right) Archive Photo, Time Pix; 11: (left) London Features, (right) Associated Press; 13: ABC TV; 52: Stephen Morley; 53 and 54: Suzanne Tenner; 55: Ron Batzdorff; 56: Sidney Baldwin; 70 (bottom): Bob Marshak; 71 (top): David Appleby; 71 (bottom): Ralph Nelson; 72: Barry Wetcher; 73 (top): Alex Baily; 77 (bottom): Mark Bellman; 83 (bottom): Nicola Goode; 84: Steven Shapiro; 88: Robbie Robinson; 89 (bottom): F. Zahedi; 91: Gemma La Mana; 92 (top): David James; 93: Sue Gordon; 100 (bottom): John Shannon; 106: Takashi Seida; 107: K. Wright; 109: Bruce McBroom; 110: Ron Batzdorff; 129 (bottom): Milton H. Greene Archives, Inc.; 136: (top) Zade Rosenthal, (bottom) Ron Batzdorff; 137: Peter Nash; 147 (bottom): Associated Press; 153 (top): Thomas D. Mcavoy, Time Pix; 153 (bottom): Las Vegas News Bureau/LVCVA; 157 (bottom): Frank Masi; 163: Sue Gordon; 169 (bottom): Las Vegas News Bureau/LVCVA; 170 (bottom): Las Vegas News Bureau/LVCVA; 171: (top) Las Vegas News Bureau/LVCVA, (bottom) Las Vegas News bureau/LVCVA; 173 (bottom): David Lee.

Published by Clarkson Potter/Publishers, New York, New York.
Member of the Crown Publishing Group, a division of Random House, Inc.
WWW.RANDOMHOUSE.COM

CLARKSON N. POTTER is a trademark and POTTER
and colophon are registered trademarks of Random House, Inc.

Printed in Singapore

DESIGN BY CAITLIN DANIELS ISRAEL

Library of Congress Cataloging-in-Publication Data
Schreier, Sandy.
Hollywood gets married / Sandy Schreier.— 1st ed.
Includes index.
1. Weddings in motion pictures. 2. Weddings in popular culture—United States. 3. Motion picture actors
and actresses—United States. I. Title

PN1995.9.M3 S37 2002
791.43'655—dc21   200154552

ISBN 0-609-80839-7

10 9 8 7 6 5 4 3 2 1

FIRST EDITION

Cover: ELIZABETH TAYLOR, *Father of the Bride,* 1950
Title page: RYAN O'NEAL, ALI MACGRAW, *Love Story,* 1970

$\mathcal{I}$ DEDICATE THIS BOOK WITH LOVE TO MY FAMILY.

Acknowledgments

I want to especially thank the people who beautify the silver screen and always have time to share their stories, their memories, and, occasionally, their secrets with me: Theoni V. Aldredge, Marit Allen, Susan Becker, Ruth Carter, Betsy Cox, Sharen Davis, Bob De Mora, Donfeld, Terry Dresbach, Melinda Eshelman, Dona Granata, Jane Greenwood, Gloria Gresham, Betsy Heimann, Lindy Hemming, Gary Jones, Michael Kaplan, Jeffrey Kurland, Mona May, Deborah Nadoolman, Rosanna Norton, Arianne Phillips, Aggie Guerard Rodgers, Ann Roth, Althea Sylbert, Kimberly Tillman, Tracy Tynan, Theadora Van Runkle, Julie Weiss, Albert Wolsky, and Michael Woulfe.

And many thanks to other helping hands: Dilys Blum, Hamish Bowles, Elizabeth Emanuel, Dale Gluckman, Titi Halle, Gary Hardwick, Anjelica Huston, Kevin Krier, Caroline Rennolds Milbank, Isaac Mizrahi, Joseph Montebello, Sarah Jessica Parker, Zandra Rhodes, Barbara Whiting Smith, Cindy Sirko, Jana Starr, and Sylvia Weinstock.

I am further indebted to those people who made this project a reality: my editor, Margot Schupf, designer Caitlin Israel, and the staff at Clarkson Potter; Bob Cosenza and Cheryl Thomas and their staffs at Kobal; Ben Carbonetta, Lou Valentino, Lauretta and Martin Dives, and especially my assistant, Suzanne Hines.

And I also dedicate this book to the memory of the designers and stars who took me into their lives and made me more starstruck than ever.

CLAUDETTE COLBERT, WALTER CONNOLLY

It Happened One Night, 1934

OFF SET

DIRECTOR: FRANK CAPRA

COSTUME DESIGNER: ROBERT KALLOCH

The wedding scene was more complicated than the public imagined. In the 1930s, it took a large crew just to hold the mike, a modern advancement compared to earlier times. According to Loretta Young, at one time small people were hired to hide behind the actresses with the fullest skirts and hold the mike atop a satin pillow, "ring-bearer style."

Contents

The author's parents,
Edward and Mollie Miller, 1930s

The author and her husband,
Sandy and Sherwin Schreier, 1950s

Introduction

WHEN I WAS A LITTLE GIRL, I DREAMED ABOUT TWO THINGS: BEING A BRIDE AND BEING A MOVIE STAR. THE FIRST PART OF MY DREAM CAME TRUE WHEN I WAS A TEENAGER, AND I AM STILL CONVINCED THAT THE MOVIE STAR PART IS JUST AROUND THE CORNER.

My parents' wedding was postponed, just hours before the ceremony, because of my father's emergency appendectomy. During his home recovery, my two uncles held up a very weak groom, clad in his best pajamas, for the nuptials. Mom and Dad's wedding portrait was taken when Daddy was fully recovered, and fifty years later Mom again wore her beautiful gown, this time slightly altered, to celebrate their golden wedding anniversary.

Hundreds of hours, thousands of dollars, and millions of tears go into one day—the wedding day—a day that passes in the blink of an eye. When I got married, hiring a wedding planner was only for the rich and famous, and because my mother wasn't a

The author's granddaughter
Celeste Schreier, 1997

detail person, I was given that responsibility. Planning my own wedding was just like producing a Broadway play or a Hollywood movie—or so I thought. I became the Ross Hunter of weddings: Ross was the movie producer who, in the fifties, brought back the lavish glamour that once was Hollywood. But he had an enormous staff and deep pockets—and I had neither.

My father was the protégé of David Nemeroff, who owned a specialty store in New York called Russeks, which carried not only ready-to-wear clothing but also French couture, furs, and precious jewels. Daddy learned the fur business and, in the thirties, was transferred to the Russeks branch in Detroit. His clientele, mostly auto barons' wives, had purchased their couture gowns in Paris prior to the war, and by the time I was old enough to visit

Dad at work, they no longer had any interest in their old clothes, which did not have the cachet they now have, plus, at that time wearing anything but American was considered unpatriotic. When I got married, I owned hundreds of pieces of French couture, all gifts from Dad's clients. These gifts were the start of my world-renowned collection, now numbering in the thousands. Over the years, I have been able to turn what once was a playtime hobby into a career that has taken me all over the world and has given me an entrée into the closets and lives of movie stars, fashion and costume designers, and the people who are fortunate enough to wear the creations designed especially for them.

Years ago, weddings were considered "grown-up affairs" and children were excluded, so young girls had to be content playing dress-up in Mom's wedding gown or wearing a mini version, now readily available. As a little girl, I thought that Hollywood costumes, designer fashion, and bridal gowns had much in common. They were my fantasy. The pomp and circumstance of a wedding were a familiar sight to me, as well as everyone else, because of the movies. Capturing the public's hearts and imaginations were the real-life "fairy princesses" of the era: from Wallis Warfield Simpson to Grace Kelly. "If they can marry a prince, then so can I" was the chant of all young girls, at least when I grew up.

For years to come, everyone talked about the king who gave up the throne for the woman he loved. The Windsors were obsessed with fashion, especially the Duchess, who explained:

The Duke and Duchess of Windsor,
June 3, 1937

Grace Kelly and Prince Rainier,
April 19, 1956

Charles and Diana,
July 29, 1981

Jack and Jackie Kennedy,
September 12, 1953

MY HUSBAND GAVE UP EVERYTHING FOR ME. I'M NOT A BEAUTIFUL WOMAN. I'M NOTHING TO LOOK AT, SO THE ONLY THING I CAN DO IS DRESS BETTER THAN ANYONE ELSE. IF EVERYONE LOOKS AT ME WHEN I ENTER A ROOM, MY HUSBAND CAN FEEL PROUD OF ME. THAT'S MY CHIEF RESPONSIBILITY.

The Duchess of Windsor's $250.00 wedding dress, designed by Mainbocher, was copied at every price and sold across the country. In New York, for example, it was sold at "swank shoppes" for $25.00, at Lord & Taylor for $16.95, and at Klein's Cash-and-Carry for $8.90.

When Grace Kelly married Prince Rainier, the American public was ecstatic. Grace, born in Philadelphia, went to Hollywood, became a star, and then moved to Monaco. Her wedding gown, by Helen Rose, used twenty-five yards of peau de soie, twenty-five yards of silk taffeta, one hundred yards of silk net, and three hundred yards of antique Valenciennes lace. Prince Rainier financed the entire wedding, including the fireworks, through the sale of postage stamps that featured his profile along with his movie-star bride.

In the eighties, when Prince Charles fell in love with Lady Diana Spencer, the world watched as the sweet and shy young woman became engaged, and everything that she did, and everything that she wore, became the most talked about subject of the day. Diana and her "mum" visited the Emanuels, who designed her wedding gown, asking that her dress reflect both the fantasy and the formality of the occasion—and also that no copies be made. According to Elizabeth Emanuel, both Diana

Julie Andrews
THE SOUND OF MUSIC, *1965*

and Prince Charles adored the finished gown, and only Miss Piggy, of Muppet fame, who owns six couture wedding gowns, has a copy.

The "royal family" title in the United States belongs to the Kennedy clan. Camelot was our own kingdom. Handsome Senator John F. Kennedy and his beautiful bride, Jacqueline Bouvier, got married in a Newport church filled with pink gladioli and white chrysanthemums. Their reception at the Auchincloss estate included a champagne dance, a cake-cutting ceremony, and a luncheon with ice-cream roses for dessert. Jackie's gown, fifty yards of ivory silk taffeta, took two months to make and was the creation of Ann Lowe, an African-American couturiere. It was too fussy for Jackie's classic taste, but she wore it to please her mother. Her jewels consisted of a simple strand of family pearls and a diamond bracelet, a wedding gift from her husband.

The weddings of the Kennedy kids also captured our hearts: first Caroline, wearing a shamrock-appliquéd Carolina Herrera gown for her marriage to Edwin Schlossberg; and ten years later, the marriage of her brother, John, to striking Carolyn Bessette. Their wedding was kept a closely guarded secret and only one image of their glorious union was released to the public: the fashionable bride, possibly about to take over where her mother-in-law had left off, wearing a minimalist Narciso Rodriguez wedding gown and not much else. But absolutely nothing else was needed: she had married the prince of Camelot.

Weddings have been in and out of fashion. But whether they are popular or not, the gowns worn by the stars have been and still are the greatest influence on the public. In years gone by, silver screen weddings, complete with bridal attire, flowers, receptions, cakes, and the like, have been seen by masses of people all over the world. Now we are influenced by the stars and their "big day," not just on the screen, but also in their real lives. Even the smallest detail is readily available on television and in magazines such as *People* and *In Style*.

For example, within hours of Jennifer Aniston's marriage to Brad Pitt, ABS (the company known for copying the celebrities' Oscar dresses) copied their first wedding gown: the $30,000 dress Jennifer wore. Future wedding trends may include kilt-wearing by grooms and babies, originating with Madonna's wedding to Guy Ritchie with kilted Baby Rocco in attendance. And Catherine Zeta-Jones may be another wedding trendsetter: sensitive to the age of many of her guests, as well as her husband, Michael Douglas, the bride had all the Plaza Hotel's lighting replaced with soft peach bulbs, giving everyone a "glow" and erasing years of wrinkles at their $1.5 million wedding. As Michael Eisner, the CEO of Disney, said:

> "PEOPLE LIKE STARS. IT'S PART OF THE CHARISMA OF THE BUSINESS. THEY LIKE TO SEE THEM. THEY LIKE TO THINK THEY CAN LOOK LIKE THEM. THEY LIKE TO THINK THEY COULD LIVE LIKE THEM."

At one time, marriages were made in heaven—today they're made by NBC. During the summer of 2000, *Today*'s online audience chose not only a bride and groom, but also selected their rings, their wedding attire, the intimates for their wedding night, and even their honeymoon destination, culminating in a wedding at Rockefeller Plaza, televised on *Today* and paid for by the network. I voted for their rings, along with 105,000 other people, and then voted for everything else as well. In 2001, those numbers more than doubled: 310,000 strong selected the bridal party's attire.

Perhaps the most famous TV wedding was in 1981, when Luke and Laura got married on *General Hospital,* a spectacle watched by 30 million viewers. Greg Kinnear, who played a soap actor in *Nurse Betty* (2000), reminisced:

> "THE MOST SOAP OPERA WATCHING I EVER DID WAS WHEN THAT WHOLE *GENERAL HOSPITAL* LUKE AND LAURA THING WAS GOING ON. I GET A LITTLE CHOKED UP JUST TALKING ABOUT IT."

Although I have spent a lifetime researching the subject of French couture and American fashion, it was the movies, the stars, and what the stars wore that filled my childhood dreams. Whenever the bride appeared, I just knew that she and her handsome husband would "live happily ever after." And when I heard those two little words, "I do," I felt as though I had just gotten married.

Luke and Laura
GENERAL HOSPITAL, *1981*

Love
IN Bloom

Just as artists glorified the bridal couples of the past, Hollywood's portrait photographers immortalized the brides of the silver screen. Long before the invention of the camera, Jan van Eyck painted *The Arnolfini Marriage* (1434), reflecting the formal pose of the bride and groom shortly after taking their vows. The color of the bride's dress is green, the sign of fertility, usually worn by brides of that period, and although her pose resembles Barbra Streisand's in *Funny Girl* (1968), it is doubtful that she is "with child," or has a pillow under her gown.

In the golden days of the silver screen (1925–1940), bridal portraiture became so popular that exorbitant amounts of talent and money were expended for that purpose. Most of the early silent films and "talkies" had brides and beautiful wedding scenes, whether or not it was called for in the story line. Formal bridal portraits were used to promote the movies and were also an important part of marketing the wedding gowns seen on the screen . . . not surprising, considering the former careers of the film industry's founders: Zukor was a furrier, Goldwyn a glove manufacturer, Fox a dress manufacturer, Mayer an antique and button dealer, and Carl Laemmle a haberdasher. When these men came to Hollywood, they didn't know how to make a movie, but they knew everything about the production and marketing of beautiful clothes.

Starting in the mid-twenties, the studios had in-house photographers and large budgets for flowers, hairdressers, and makeup artists to enhance each bridal shot. The costume designer not only worked on dozens of films and designed the stars' at-home attire, but, at the same time, designed the wedding gowns for the publicity photos. They worked around the clock with cutters, seamstresses, beaders, and embroiderers to entice the public with their spectacular creations. And enticed they were: 65 percent of the public saw at least one movie per week in the thirties, as opposed to in the late seventies, when that figure dropped to only 10 percent because of the popularity of television.

Young starlets were in great demand for wedding portraits, which appeared in fan magazines such as *Modern Screen* and *Photoplay*. These pictures whetted the public's appetite for stars and stories and also promoted the starlets' careers. The bigger the star, the more extravagant the wedding gown: the $100,000 wedding gowns worn by both Pola Negri in *The Cheat* (1923) and Gloria Swanson in *Her Love Story* (1924); a Venetian wedding gown made from 185 yards of satin and lace for Marion Davies in *Cain and Mabel* (1936); and Norma Shearer's wedding gown in *Marie Antoinette* (1938), which weighed as much as Norma—110 pounds. These gowns, publicity-wise, were worth their weight in gold.

In 1937, Hollywood's wedding frenzy inspired the Basil Rathbones to make a "bride and groom" party, which was covered extensively by *Life* magazine. Guests were expected to dress as famous couples on their wedding day. Marlene Dietrich came dressed as a groom, wearing a tuxedo, a look for women that she originated; and costume designer Gwen Wakeling created a gown for Loretta Young: "I made her the bride from hell, 'Satan's Bride,' with sequined horns and a black veil. I was delighted when she won first prize."

Previous page

JEAN ARTHUR, 1930
PHOTO BY EUGENE ROBERT RICHEE

🌣

Squeaky-voiced Jean Arthur played mostly lackluster roles until *The Whole Town's Talking* in 1935. Because wedding portraiture was so popular, studios often had new starlets, like Jean, pose in wedding gowns, but it wasn't often that a portrait would become an image that the public worshiped and other photographers copied. Such was the case with this photo. Photographer Eugene Robert Richee always shot the stars in the fashion of the day, and was the first studio photographer to shoot Gary Cooper and also Marlene Dietrich.

CLARA BOW

❧

Her Wedding Night, 1930
DIRECTOR: FRANK TUTTLE

This film was made during the last popular year of the "It Girl's" career. The Jazz Age was being replaced by puritanical times, and the gossip about Clara Bow's "entertaining" the entire USC football team didn't sit well with the public. Also, silent films were being replaced by the talkies, and Bow's heavy Brooklyn accent was of great concern to the front office. Virginal publicity shots didn't seem to help Clara Bow's declining popularity.

MIRIAM HOPKINS

Design for Living, 1933

DIRECTOR: ERNST LUBITSCH
COSTUME DESIGNER: TRAVIS BANTON

This film was based on Noel Coward's supposedly autobiographical play of the same title. It's the story of two best friends, Fredric March and Gary Cooper, who both fall in love with Paris and with Miriam Hopkins. Miriam marries Edward Everett Horton for security, but after both Fred and Gary send flowers to her suite, she runs off with the two of them. Hopkins's beautiful wedding gown was designed by Travis Banton, who also created daring costumes for Dietrich and Cleopatra couture for Colbert.

SYLVIA SIDNEY

❧

Merrily We Go to Hell, 1932
DIRECTOR: DOROTHY ARZNER

Sylvia Sidney marries Fredric March, a struggling playwright, who finally writes a hit and then falls for another woman. But he's an alcoholic, so what did she expect? This comedy was directed by Dorothy Arzner, one of the few female directors in the early days of the studio system. She edited the bullfight scenes in Valentino's *Blood and Sand* (1922) and directed Katharine Hepburn in *Christopher Strong* (1933). Dorothy continued working for many years, teaching film students at UCLA, including Francis Ford Coppola, and producing Pepsi commercials for her good friend Joan Crawford.

JOAN CRAWFORD

❧

Dancing Lady, 1933
DIRECTOR: ROBERT Z. LEONARD
COSTUME DESIGNER: ADRIAN

In *Dancing Lady*, Fred Astaire makes his screen debut with Joan Crawford as his partner. Before Hollywood, Joan began her career as a dancer in the "hot spots" of Detroit and Chicago. The film's plot centers around a love triangle between Crawford, Clark Gable, and Franchot Tone, who became Joan's third husband. Her costumes were designed by MGM's star designer, Adrian, who was responsible for most of the screen fashion trends of the thirties, including Joan's shoulder-padded look. Crawford said that working with him was the turning point of her career; that until him, she didn't know one thing about dressing—or undressing, for that matter.

CLAUDETTE COLBERT

❦

It Happened One Night, 1934
DIRECTOR: FRANK CAPRA
COSTUME DESIGNER: ROBERT KALLOCH

Clark Gable's lack of underwear was the highlight of this film, causing many men's furnishings buyers to lose their jobs. If the King didn't wear an undershirt, neither would any red-blooded American male! In this film, thinking that reporter Clark Gable has deserted her, heiress Claudette Colbert returns home to marry a society aviator, wearing a showstopping wedding gown. The costumes were designed by Robert Kalloch, who was hired by studio head Harry Cohn to make sure all his stars looked stylish. Harry hated period films, saying that "the clothes looked dated."

PAULETTE GODDARD, 1936

✵

PUBLICITY STILL

Paulette Goddard was a Ziegfeld Girl at the age of thirteen, a married woman at sixteen, and a divorced one the following year. Later, in 1931, she went to Hollywood, where she met and married Charlie Chaplin. This publicity shot for a Laurel and Hardy comedy was released to the public shortly after the Chaplins' shipboard wedding. Paulette appeared in two of Charlie's films: *Modern Times* (1936) and *The Great Dictator* (1940). When she married him, she was nineteen and he was an "old man" of forty-four. Paulette was Charlie's third wife — his last was Oona O'Neill, who was seventeen when she married the fifty-four-year-old filmmaker. They had eight children together.

MARGARET SULLAVAN

The Good Fairy, 1935
DIRECTOR: WILLIAM WYLER
COSTUME DESIGNER: VERA WEST

Luisa Ginglebusher (Margaret Sullavan) leaves an orphanage to become a movie usherette, promising the children left behind that she'll come back as "the good fairy." Both Margaret and screenwriter Preston Sturges were from wealthy socialite families. Margaret was immediately drawn to the theater, but Preston first managed his mother's cosmetic company in France and, after World War I, invented a kissproof lipstick. He was the sophisticated humorist who wrote *The Lady Eve* (1941) and *The Palm Beach Story* (1942), two films with extraordinary wedding scenes. Margaret's three husbands were producer Leland Hayward, Henry Fonda, and the director of this film, William Wyler.

BETTY GRABLE

❊

This Way, Please, 1937
DIRECTOR: ROBERT FLOREY
COSTUME DESIGNER: EDITH HEAD

In 1937, Betty Grable, America's most famous pinup girl, was an aspiring star and married to Jackie Coogan, a former child star. After many years of small films such as this one, a new studio and luscious Technicolor showed off both her talent and her beauty. Betty's legs— or "gams," as they were called—were insured by Lloyds of London for a million dollars. Her wedding veil is embroidered with shiny cellophane, a concept developed by Edith Head, the screen's most prolific designer, who began creating costumes in the thirties and continued until her death in 1981.

GINGER ROGERS

❀

Carefree, 1938
DIRECTOR: MARK SANDRICH
COSTUME DESIGNER: HOWARD GREER

In most of the Astaire-Rogers musicals, Fred and Ginger dance off into feather-featherland, but it's rare to see them actually getting married; and, because Fred's wife, Phyllis, was opposed to his kissing Ginger, this is one of their rare screen kisses. In the real world, each of Ginger's five marriages lasted no more than five years. Her "marriage" to Fred lasted sixteen. Before designing film costumes, Howard Greer worked in Paris and London with some of fashion's greatest couturieres: Lucille, Poiret, and Molyneux.

MERLE OBERON

❀

Wuthering Heights, 1939
DIRECTOR: WILLIAM WYLER
COSTUME DESIGNER: OMAR KIAM

This Oscar-winning picture was based on Emily Brontë's novel of doomed love in Victorian England. Producer Samuel Goldwyn transformed 450 acres in California into the English moors. He also switched the novel's period from Regency to Georgian, allowing Merle Oberon to wear much more opulent costumes and show off her beautiful shoulders. During the wedding ceremony, the groom, played by David Niven, was very nervous and said, "I've never been married before." Shortly before filming began, he and Merle were a couple.

MAUREEN O'HARA

❧

How Green Was My Valley, 1941
DIRECTOR: JOHN FORD
COSTUME DESIGNER: GWEN WAKELING

This is the story of a Welsh coal-mining family with "Master" Roddy McDowall, the youngest child, telling the story. Director John Ford's masterpiece stood up to *Citizen Kane,* another Oscar nominee, by winning the Academy Award for Best Picture that year. This film seems to be shot through a layer of coal dust, except when Maureen O'Hara is on the screen. Perhaps best remembered for *Miracle on 34th Street,* the Dublin-born beauty was radiant throughout, especially in her wedding gown.

BETTE DAVIS

The Old Maid, 1939

DIRECTOR: EDMUND GOULDING
COSTUME DESIGNER: ORRY-KELLY

This movie centered on love and hate and jealousy in the late nineteenth century, together with beautiful wedding gowns, the first of which was worn by Bette Davis. Her costar Miriam Hopkins also wears a beautiful wedding gown, and there were loud fights between the stars as to who would wear the best one. Orry-Kelly designed most of the Davis movies, minimizing her many figure faults and reminding her to wear a bra—Bette never did—which was definitely a necessity for period costuming. This movie has four weddings and also handsome George Brent, who appeared with Bette in eleven movies in eleven years.

MARLENE DIETRICH

❧

The Flame of New Orleans, 1941
DIRECTOR: RENÉ CLAIR
COSTUME DESIGNER: RENÉ HUBERT

The trailer for this film says it all:

> A beautiful adventuress arrives in New
> Orleans from Paris. Her wedding dress
> was found floating in the river…
> NATURALLY…A MAN WAS TO BLAME!!

Marlene's mysterious sex appeal lost its popularity
during the war years, when a foreign accent became
suspect. She ignored Hitler's invitations to return to
Germany. Instead, she went to entertain U.S. troops.
She also changed her persona and selected more
comedic roles. Answering the rumors about her
many love affairs, Marlene said, "In Europe, it does-
n't matter if you're a man or a woman—we make love
with anyone we find attractive."

GENE TIERNEY

❧

The Razor's Edge, 1946
DIRECTOR: EDMUND GOULDING
COSTUME DESIGNER: OLEG CASSINI

Clifton Webb's obsession with Gene Tierney in *Laura*
(1944) is repeated in this film. In one scene, Webb,
with that lecherous sneer, says, "Pretty dress she had
on … I hadn't realized it was cut quite so low." Of
course he noticed her dress; it was designed by her
husband, Oleg Cassini, who also designed many of
Jackie Kennedy's clothes during her White House
years. Gene suffered from mental and physical condi-
tions—in particular, an eye problem that gave her a
Far Eastern look, and a breakdown brought on by the
sudden end of her romance with Aly Khan.

ANN SOTHERN

❧

Panama Hattie, 1942
DIRECTOR: NORMAN Z. MCLEOD
COSTUME DESIGNER: ROBERT KALLOCH

Ann Sothern played Maisie, the scatterbrained blond heroine in ten films, but she didn't get the opportunity to show off her musical comedy talent until *Panama Hattie.* An uncredited Vincente Minnelli directed, wrote, and choreographed the screen adaptation. In the fifties, Ann was the star of her own TV shows: *Private Secretary* and *The Ann Sothern Show.* She was nominated for an Oscar as best supporting actress for her role in *The Whales of August* in 1987.

KATHARINE HEPBURN

❧

The Philadelphia Story, 1940
DIRECTOR: GEORGE CUKOR
COSTUME DESIGNER: ADRIAN

Hepburn appeared in the Broadway play *The Philadelphia Story,* the lead having been written especially for her, and instead of a salary, she took a cut of the profits. Kate also owned the film's adaptation rights, which she later sold to Louis B. Mayer for a large profit and the right to select the cast and crew. She chose George Cukor, who was known as the woman's director of MGM; and, as her costume designer, she chose Adrian, who dressed her in feminine clothes unlike the usual slacks and roll-sleeved shirts she loved to wear. Both of these men were her good friends.

LANA TURNER

Marriage Is a Private Affair, 1944

DIRECTOR: ROBERT Z. LEONARD

COSTUME DESIGNER: IRENE

Lana, known as Hollywood's "Sweater Girl," was a favorite pinup during World War II. Before her film career, she dreamed of becoming a fashion designer, which explains her interest in every detail of her wardrobe, both on and off the screen. Her 1948 wedding to Bob Topping was delayed because she made changes to her trousseau that were, according to designer Don Loper, unerringly correct.

ELIZABETH TAYLOR

✵

Father of the Bride, 1950
DIRECTOR: VINCENTE MINNELLI
COSTUME DESIGNER: HELEN ROSE

Oh, that we could all be members of the Banks family: Spencer Tracy as the sweet and sincere dad, Joan Bennett as the soft-spoken mom, and Billie Burke as ditsy Doris Dunston, the mother-in-law. Is there any young girl planning a wedding, real or imaginary, who doesn't yearn to look like Liz Taylor in this movie, and have the opportunity to wear a Helen Rose wedding gown? For one lucky person that dream became a reality—the successful bidder for *The Father of the Bride* wedding gown at the MGM auction of props and costumes in May 1970.

SOPHIA LOREN

❧

Houseboat, 1958

DIRECTOR: MELVILLE SHAVELSON
COSTUME DESIGNER: EDITH HEAD

In this movie, Cary Grant, a widower with three young children, hires a nanny, who is really an Italian socialite running away from her overbearing father. Gorgeous Sophia is the star; no wonder Cary fell. Sophia grew up outside Naples and married Carlo Ponti, who is twenty-two years her senior. When asked about her appeal, she said, "Sex appeal is fifty percent what you've got and fifty percent what people think you've got."

VIRNA LISI

✣

Better a Widow (Meglio Vedova), 1969
DIRECTOR: DUCCIO TESSARI
COSTUME DESIGNER: ADRIANA BERSELLI

In the fifties, Virna Lisi played in cheap melodramas, but during the sixties, she became an international star. Could the reason have been the mod clothes that suited her so beautifully? By the late sixties, the youth culture was not only on the streets and catwalks but also on the silver screen, its influence even reaching bridal attire.

GINA LOLLOBRIGIDA

ℳ

Stuntman (Le Cascadeur), 1968
DIRECTOR: MARCELLO BALDI
(AKA BILLY MARSHALL)

Called "the Most Beautiful Woman in the World," Gina was a finalist in the Miss Italy contest, which led to the start of her film career. Her tossed-salad hairdo became world renowned (it was called the "Italian" in the United States) and a type of lettuce was named "Lollo" in honor of Gina's hairdo. Another generation was introduced to Lollobrigida when she appeared on TV's *Falcon Crest* in the eighties.

BO DEREK

10, 1979

DIRECTOR: BLAKE EDWARDS
COSTUME DESIGNER: PATRICIA EDWARDS

Dudley Moore, having a midlife crisis, stops for a red light and sees a limo carrying Bo Derek, a gorgeous young woman on the way to her wedding. He falls instantly, crashes her wedding, stalks her on her honeymoon, and strikes gold. Moore saves her husband's life and, in return, gets Bo, braids, and *Bolero* (Ravel, that is).

JESSICA LANGE

❧

Everybody's All–American, 1988
DIRECTOR: TAYLOR HACKFORD
COSTUME DESIGNER: THEADORA VAN RUNKLE

This film relates the twenty-five-year saga of a football hero and a prom queen. The beautiful wedding gown was designed by Theadora Van Runkle, who had to make certain adjustments to the dress because Jessica Lange was nursing her third child. Theadora made the fashion world sit up and take notice when she costumed *Bonnie and Clyde* (1967) and also *The Thomas Crown Affair*, the original, in 1968.

"Betty Grable and Harry James! Folks think those two were born joined at the hip or born married. But before she was his wife, she was mine."
— Jackie Coogan (TV's Uncle Fester)

ALWAYS A *Bridesmaid*

Shortly before Grace Kelly's marriage to His Serene Highness Prince Rainier III, she addressed her bridesmaids: "Having all of you here with me today makes all the difference in the world."

The white wedding, as we know it today, is a trend that started with Queen Victoria in 1840. But Hollywood brides and their bridesmaids never wore white in the early films, as it created a glare on the screen; instead, their gowns were pale pink or pale blue. Similarly, early American brides and their attendants wore pastel colors, as it was customary for the bridesmaid to match the bride.

At one time, the brides were so young that older women in the village would help them dress, providing guidance for the wedding night—and smelling salts when necessary. They were called "the bride's helpers." They also made floral wreaths for the bridal party and even offered to stand in for the bride to ward off the evil spirits. None of these traditions are pictured in Hollywood movies.

Instead, the bridesmaids of the silver screen, before the sixties, were always perfect: perfectly young, perfectly tall and slender, and perfectly beautiful. Before filming began on *They All Kissed the Bride* (1942), there was a casting call for eight same height, identically built girls to play the part of the bridesmaids. Acting ability was not a prerequisite.

Florenz Ziegfeld gave the *Ziegfeld Follies* bridesmaids something to do. In *Funny Girl* (1968), the story of Fanny Brice, who began her career in the *Follies,* the tall, scantily dressed bridesmaids recite the following ditty:

> *The winter bride is typified by Christmas frost and fairies*
> *And though the winter's changeable, her virtue never varies*
>
> *The springtime bride is starry-eyed as poets often say*
> *No other bride would ever dare to dream the dreams that April May*
>
> *The summer bride is glorified by Merlin's magic touch*
> *A lucky man receives the love of June, July, and such*
>
> *The autumn bride is prudent and wise at sweet sixteen or twenty*
> *And as a wife in future life, she'll hold the horn of plenty*

At real weddings, the bridal attendants are expected to look beautiful and act happy. But why are they happy? They have to stand in a lineup with other women who are wearing the identical dress, which they all pay for themselves and will never wear again!

Previous page

JOAN CRAWFORD

᷑

They All Kissed the Bride, 1942

OFF SET

DIRECTOR: ALEXANDER HALL
COSTUME DESIGNER: IRENE

Joan Crawford plays a career woman who yearns for knitting and babies. She's the older sister of the bride and her maid of honor. Carole Lombard was first cast in Joan's part, but was killed in a plane crash shortly before filming was to begin. Crawford contributed her entire salary to the American Red Cross in Carole's memory.

GLORIA SWANSON

✺

Haystacks and Steeples, 1916
DIRECTOR: CLARENCE BADGER

While working as a movie extra in 1913, Gloria Swanson met her first husband, actor Wallace Beery, who was hired by Mack Sennett's Keystone company on the condition that it also hire Gloria. She was never a slapstick performer, but appeared in romantic comedies such as this. Gloria married and divorced very often, once to royalty. Swanson is best known for her comeback role in *Sunset Boulevard* (1950). Unlike Norma Desmond, Gloria continued to lead an active life, later founding a cosmetics business and a dress company for mature women.

Left to right: JACK CONWAY, ISABELLA CROWDIN,
DOUGLAS SHEARER, MARION DAVIES, NORMA SHEARER,
IRVING THALBERG, ROSABELLE LAEMMLE, LOUIS B. MAYER,
IRENE MAYER, EDITH MAYER, KING VIDOR

❧

WEDDING OF NORMA SHEARER AND IRVING G. THALBERG,
SEPTEMBER 29, 1927

"The Boy Wonder" of MGM married one of its biggest stars—and his boss, Louis B. Mayer, was his best man. Sounds like a fairy tale, but Irving G. Thalberg, responsible for Hollywood's "dream factory," was in fact a very sickly young man who died from heart problems at the age of thirty-seven. When he married Norma Shearer, she became the "queen of the lot" and was allowed to select the best costumes, usually in white satin, which designer Adrian referred to as "Norma's nighties." Mayer paid for the Thalbergs' wedding and honeymoon, but the honeymoon with Mayer was short-lived when Irving became ill and his power was stripped away.

MARION DAVIES

⌖

Show People, 1928
DIRECTOR: KING VIDOR
COSTUME DESIGNER: HENRIETTA FRAZER

This movie is a must for film and fashion buffs—not only for the stylish twenties' clothes, but cameo appearances by Charlie Chaplin, Douglas Fairbanks, John Gilbert, Elinor Glyn (who wrote *It,* 1927), director King Vidor, and Mae Murray. Marion Davies, who produced *Show People,* was the longtime paramour of William Randolph Hearst. Her costar was William Haines, Hollywood's first openly gay star. Louis B. Mayer threatened to fire Haines if he refused to drop his lover, but love prevailed. Joan Crawford called them "the happiest married couple in America."

"Marriage is a great institution.
I'm not ready for an institution."
—Mae West

LORETTA YOUNG, MAID OF HONOR,
JUNE 28, 1933

The ever-fashionable Loretta Young served as maid of honor
at the marriage of John Wayne and Josephine Saenz, daughter
of the Panamanian consul, in Los Angeles. The ceremony was
performed in Loretta's Bel Air home, but the marriage ended in
divorce in 1945. Loretta is carrying a flower-covered muff, so
popular in the 1930s.

ROSALIND RUSSELL, WALTER PIDGEON, MYRNA LOY

❧

Man-Proof, 1938

DIRECTOR: RICHARD THORPE
COSTUME DESIGNER: DOLLY TREE

Both Roz and Myrna are in love with Walter, but he chooses Roz, who, in her medieval bridal headdress, looks as if she is about to take a vow of celibacy. No wonder Walter reconsidered. Dolly Tree, the costume designer, created costumes for twelve films at the same time as *Man-Proof*—not an unusual feat for a costume designer at that time.

CAROLE LOMBARD, NAT PENDLETON

❧

The Gay Bride, 1934
DIRECTOR: JACK CONWAY
COSTUME DESIGNER: DOLLY TREE

Carole Lombard said, "I've lived by a man's code, designed to fit a man's world, yet, at the same time, I never forget that a woman's first job is to choose the right shade of lipstick." In this crime comedy, Carole plays a gold-digging showgirl looking for a gangster to love.

RITA HAYWORTH, CATHERINE CRAIG, ADOLPH MENJOU

✺

You Were Never Lovelier, 1942

DIRECTOR: WILLIAM A. SEITER

COSTUME DESIGNER: IRENE

Rita, one of four daughters, was her older sister's maid of honor. According to Daddy, Adolphe Menjou, she has to get married next, before her two younger sisters. Menjou selects his daughter's wedding gown and trousseau because he "has such good taste." He was considered one of the silver screen's snappiest dressers. Rita's singing was dubbed in this film, but her dancing with Fred Astaire was never lovelier, although she wore small heels because of Fred's insecurity about his height.

DEANNA DURBIN AND BRIDESMAIDS AT HER 1941 MARRIAGE TO PRODUCER VAUGHAN PAUL

In 1939, at the age of eighteen, Deanna Durbin was the highest-paid star in the world, making $250,000 a year. She was the queen of licensing agreements: there were Durbin dolls, dresses, and even houses promising that the buyer would live "happily ever after." Durbin saved Universal Studios from financial disaster with her bubbly personality and upbeat songs. She retired from the screen in 1948 and lives with her third husband in France.

WEDDING OF JOHN AGAR AND SHIRLEY TEMPLE,
SEPTEMBER 19, 1945

❧

All little girls wanted to be Shirley Temple! Shirley tap-danced, sang, had curls and dimples, and was beloved all over the world. For three years during the thirties, she was America's top box office draw, even winning a special Oscar in recognition of her outstanding contribution to the film industry. But, alas, Shirley grew up, became an awkward teenager, and even got married. In 1948, she appeared in a John Ford film as an ingénue opposite her husband, John Agar. The film was a failure and so was the marriage. She has been married to Charles Black since 1950.

BETTY HUTTON

❧

Dream Girl, 1948
DIRECTOR: MITCHELL LEISEN
COSTUME DESIGNER: EDITH HEAD

Betty Hutton appears as the maid of honor at her sister's wedding, all dressed up in buttons and bows. Betty is a daydreamer, sort of a Walter Mitty type—with a crush on her new brother-in-law. She imagines various scenarios for weddings, and in each one she is married to her sister's husband. At one point, Mom says to the groom, "Hurry up, young man. You're holding up a $5,800 wedding!"

SUZY PARKER, DIANE VARSI

❧

Ten North Frederick, 1958
DIRECTOR: PHILIP DUNNE
COSTUME DESIGNER: CHARLES LE MAIRE

Suzy Parker, one of the greatest fashion models of the fifties, appeared in nine films, including *Funny Face* (1957), the story of the fashion industry. In *Ten North Frederick*, fifty-seven-year-old Gary Cooper is her love interest. The year before, audiences protested the older man/younger woman syndrome when Gary appeared with twenty-eight-year-old Audrey Hepburn in *Love in the Afternoon*. Ingrid Bergman said, "Every woman who knew him fell in love with Gary"—no matter the age!

ROBERT DE NIRO, JOHN SAVAGE, CHRISTOPHER WALKEN,
MERYL STREEP, AND FRIENDS

The Deer Hunter, 1978

DIRECTOR: MICHAEL CIMINO
COSTUME DESIGNERS: SANDY BERKE AND ERIC SEELIG

The Deer Hunter is an epic story of Pennsylvania steelworkers: their lives, their loves, and their time served in Vietnam. The movie also has a one-hour wedding, complete with old-world traditions such as the grandmothers carrying the cake and the bride and groom's candle ceremony, and some newer traditions—such as a pregnant bride.

JILL EIKENBERRY, DUDLEY MOORE

Arthur, 1981

DIRECTOR: STEVE GORDON
COSTUME DESIGNER: JANE GREENWOOD

Arthur, played by Dudley Moore, will lose his estate of $750 million unless he marries Susan (Jill Eikenberry), whom he doesn't love. Designer Jane Greenwood recalled that just a few hours before the shoot, Moore's trailer, parked on New York's Upper East Side, was broken into and his entire custom wardrobe was stolen. In the film, on the way to the wedding, Dudley stops at Bergdorf's and buys four dozen green sweaters; but in reality, it was the entire wedding party that stopped off at Bergdorf's for the gorgeous gowns. The wedding was still a no-go. Too bad—Jill and the bridesmaids looked fabulous!

MOLLY RINGWALD, CARLIN GLYNN

Sixteen Candles, 1984

DIRECTOR: JOHN HUGHES
COSTUME DESIGNER: MARLA DENISE SCHLOM

On her sister's wedding day, everyone has forgotten that it's Molly's sixteenth birthday. Although Molly is pretty in pink, the real scene stealers are Joan Cusack, wearing a neckbrace, and the stoned bride, trying to eat the rice as it's being thrown.

"It's bloody impractical: to love, honor and obey. If it weren't, you wouldn't have to sign a contract."
—Katharine Hepburn

HUGH GRANT, CHARLOTTE COLEMAN

Four Weddings and a Funeral, 1994

DIRECTOR: MIKE NEWELL

COSTUME DESIGNER: LINDY HEMMING

If you love weddings, formal attire, bridesmaids, flowers, music, wedding cakes, and toasts, you can OD on this film, as of 1999 the highest-grossing British film in cinema history. Costume designer Lindy Hemming said that she followed the screenwriter's description of Grant's character: "always late, never prepared, and messy." But, Lindy said, "it was hard to make Hugh Grant look any way but perfect. Since his character wasn't thrilled about being at these weddings, he waits until the last minute and either borrows a tux from a friend, or hires something from Moss Bros, the Englishman's answer to formalwear. Hugh doesn't bother with a proper fitting; he's a phone-in order."

JULIA ROBERTS, CAMERON DIAZ

My Best Friend's Wedding, 1997
DIRECTOR: P. J. HOGAN
COSTUME DESIGNER: JEFFREY KURLAND

The bride, played by Cameron Diaz, says to Julia Roberts as she tries on her bridesmaid's dress, "He's got you on a pedestal and me in his arms." Designer Jeffrey Kurland, who had everyone talking about the sexy office attire he created for Julia's *Erin Brockovich* (2000) look, made six copies of this dress: four unfinished ones for the fitting scene and two for the wedding, complete with couture details such as handmade flowers. In the film, the fitter tells Julia that "the dress is going to be tighter . . . you don't want those things falling out." She wasn't referring to Julia's compact and lipstick!

ASHLEY JUDD, NATALIE PORTMAN, JAMES FRAIN

❦

Where the Heart Is, 2000

DIRECTOR: MATT WILLIAMS

COSTUME DESIGNER: MELINDA ESHELMAN

Natalie plays a very pregnant seventeen-year-old whose boyfriend dumps her at a Wal-Mart in Oklahoma, where she delivers her baby. Her wedding gown was ordered from a bridal catalog, but because the shoot was moved up, the costume designer had to produce the gown overnight—beadwork, crystals, and all—with very little help. Ashley's bridesmaid dress is authentic: lavender acetate, with a baby bunting to match. Her six kids in the movie are all named after junk food (Brownie, Praline, Baby Ruth, etc.). All of that sugar and spice was contagious: the costume designer delivered her own "snack pack" nine months later.

JOAN CUSACK, JULIA ROBERTS, KATHLEEN MARSHALL

※

Runaway Bride, 1999
DIRECTOR: GARRY MARSHALL
COSTUME DESIGNER: ALBERT WOLSKY

Maggie Carpenter (Julia Roberts)—always a bride, never a bridesmaid—her wedding jitters being comforted and calmed by her attendants. Those two lucky girls have lots of Albert Wolsky–designed bridesmaid dresses, a different one for each of Julia's weddings. Most bridesmaids lose it when they see the first one! Albert won Oscars for *All That Jazz* (1979) and *Bugsy* (1990) and has received five Academy Award nominations. He also received the Lifetime Achievement award from the Costume Designer's Guild for his impressive film career, beginning with *The Heart Is a Lonely Hunter* in 1968.

IT TAKES *Two*

THE SIGNIFICANCE OF THE MARRIAGE CEREMONY AND THE
LOVE BETWEEN THE BRIDE AND GROOM IS ALWAYS THE SAME,
WHETHER ON SCREEN OR OFF. IN HOLLYWOOD, IT BEGINS WITH
THE BRIDE AND THE COSTUME DESIGNER, WHO DEVELOP A RELA-
TIONSHIP THAT IS SYNONYMOUS WITH A MOTHER AND DAUGHTER,
SHOPPING FOR THE BIG DAY AND "THE MOST IMPORTANT DRESS OF
A LIFETIME." THE SCREEN BRIDE, IN HER GLORIOUS WEDDING
GOWN, WILL NOT ONLY BE SEEN BY FRIENDS AND FAMILY, BUT BY
THE WHOLE WORLD. THE ACTORS PORTRAYING THE "HAPPY COU-
PLE," TOGETHER WITH THE CAST AND THE CREW, WHOSE WARM
FEELINGS HAVE ENVELOPED THE SET, HOPE TO MAKE THIS FAN-
TASY WEDDING THE MOST MAGICAL MOMENT OF THE MOVIE.

Unlike bridal designers, whose ideas are somewhat limited—from
minimalist sheaths to opulent "princess" gowns—in Hollywood, when a
costume designer creates a wedding gown, the sky's the limit. British-
born Marit Allen (*Eyes Wide Shut,* 1999) recalls that as a young girl, she
read American magazines and dreamed about the brides in the ads, and
those memories have been the inspiration for the wedding gowns she
has designed for the movies. And Julie Weiss (*American Beauty,* 1999)
expressed her sentiments about her designs for two of Hollywood's
favorite brides, Julia Roberts in *Steel Magnolias* (1989) and Sarah Jessica
Parker in *Honeymoon in Vegas* (1992):

> WHAT A GLORIOUS OPPORTUNITY TO DESIGN A WEDDING GOWN.
> IT IS SOMETHING THAT I WOULD IMAGINE EVERY COSTUME
> DESIGNER LONGS FOR—A DRESS WITH A TRAIN CARRYING YEARS
> OF TRADITION AND NEW BEGINNINGS FOR THE BRIDE AND HER
> COMMUNITY—YARDS AND YARDS OF SILK AND LACE HOLDING
> ONE'S FAMILY FOOTPRINTS.

THE WEDDING GOWN IN STEEL MAGNOLIAS, WORN BY JULIA ROBERTS, WAS BORN FROM A CIVIL WAR DRESS: A TIGHTLY FITTED BODICE, A HOOP, A BUSTLE, A CRINOLINE, AND, OF COURSE, A BOW. SCRIPTED AS A DRESS OF "BASHFUL PINK," JULIA'S DRESS WAS A CONTINUATION OF THE BRIDAL BOUQUET, OVERFLOWING WITH CASCADES OF THE PALEST OF PINK-AND-IVORY SILK SATIN MAGNO-LIAS, LONG-STEM ROSES, VELVET PETALS, AND AN OCCASIONAL THORN, ALL HANDMADE WITH SATIN, ORGANDY, AND CHIFFON. THE BRIDE'S COURT WERE ALL SOUTHERN BELLES, SWATHED IN EVEN MORE LAYERS OF PINK ON PINK ON PINK.

IN HONEYMOON IN VEGAS, THE BRIDESMAIDS WERE THE "FLYING ELVISES," WHO FORMED AN AERIAL EMBRACE IN HONOR OF THE BRIDE, SARAH JESSICA PARKER. HER BRIDAL DRESS WAS A LAS VEGAS SHOWGIRL COSTUME, WITH ONLY THE MINIMUM DOSAGE OF BRIDAL GOWN REQUIRED—A HEADDRESS, A VEIL, A CORSET, A G-STRING, A GARTER, A TRAIN, AND MAGICAL SLIPPERS. THE COSTUME, GILDED WITH BEJEWELED PETALS AND VINES, SOMEHOW LOOKED AS IF IT HAD BEEN SHOWERED WITH THE FLO-RAL DUSTINGS OF THE STEEL MAGNOLIAS WEDDING PARTY: A COM-BINATION ONLY THIS BRIDE COULD CARRY OFF IN SUCH A LOVING MANNER.

Previous page

COURTNEY LOVE, WOODY HARRELSON

᭶

The People vs. Larry Flynt, 1996
DIRECTOR: MILOS FORMAN
COSTUME DESIGNER: ARIANNE PHILLIPS

The real Larry Flynt told director Milos Forman, "Whatever you need to do, just do it." The costume designer, Arianne Phillips, who is best known as Madonna's stylist, said that although the real Flynt wedding was "peachy," she used red for drama but "stayed true to the period." The wedding looks like a big Valentine: red and white and romantic all over. It's hard to believe that this was the wedding of subculture smut leader Larry Flynt and his wild girlfriend, Althea!

BEVERLY BAYNE,
FRANCIS X. BUSHMAN

❧

Under Royal Patronage, 1914
DIRECTOR: E. H. CALVERT

Handsome Francis X. Bushman first worked as an artist's model before becoming Hollywood's romantic lead in almost two hundred films—forty in 1914 alone. Although he won *The Ladies' World* hero contest, his career lost momentum when his secret marriage to costar Beverly Bayne was discovered. Their most popular film was *Romeo and Juliet* (1916).

NORMA TALMADGE,
EUGENE O'BRIEN

❧

The Only Woman, 1924
DIRECTOR: SIDNEY OLCOTT

Norma Talmadge was one of three sisters who were all popular in Hollywood's early days. The youngest, Constance, appeared in D. W. Griffith's *Intolerance* (1916) and was almost as successful as Norma. Sister Natalie was more famous as Buster Keaton's wife. This is one of Norma's last films, as her voice was not adaptable to the talkies. Her second husband was comedian George Jessel, whose radio show and marriage to Norma both failed in 1939.

W. C. FIELDS, MAE WEST

ৎৡ

My Little Chickadee, 1940
DIRECTOR: EDWARD F. CLINE
COSTUME DESIGNER: VERA WEST

Mae West made only twelve films in her forty-six-year career, but in all of them, she pushed our buttons making fun of a then-puritanical society. In 1926, she wrote a play called *Sex,* which landed her in jail on obscenity charges. West hated the Hollywood costume designers, who were forever trying to minimize her "figure faults." Mae's figure did not fit the mold of the silver-screen standard; she wanted it to be maximized instead of minimized. Although Flower Belle Lee (Mae) and Cuthbert J. Twillie (W.C.) pretended to be married, in the real world, West thought that Fields was a "crude slob" and had no use for him—other than to help her write this screenplay.

WILLIAM HOLDEN, MARTHA SCOTT, GUY KIBBEE

Our Town, 1940

DIRECTOR: SAM WOOD

COSTUME DESIGNER: EDWARD P. LAMBERT

Martha Scott landed her first role on the Broadway stage as the lead in *Our Town* in 1938. She re-created the role of Emily in the screen adaptation. Her costar Bill Holden became a box office sensation in *Golden Boy* (1939). When he married Brenda Marshall in 1941, he and his best man, Brian Donlevy, were filming and didn't arrive at the service until 3:00 A.M.; it wasn't until 4:00 that a Las Vegas preacher could be found. They left immediately to resume shooting. Three months later, Bill and Brenda finally went on their honeymoon; previous plans had been canceled when both the bride and the groom underwent emergency appendectomies!

GEORGE MURPHY, GINGER ROGERS

❧

Tom, Dick and Harry, 1941
DIRECTOR: GARSON KANIN
COSTUME DESIGNER: RENIE

In *Tom, Dick and Harry*, Ginger dreams of marrying all three men. In one dream, the bride and groom look like cake toppers. After the ceremony, Ginger does kitchen duty wearing a daisy-covered dress that matches her curtains. She had a total of forty-five costumes, including a wedding gown made from flour sacks. Costume designer Renie designed Ginger's wardrobe for *Kitty Foyle* (1940), which to this day sets the standard for workingwomen's attire. Ginger won the Oscar saying "My first role was Kitty Foyle—that person dancing with Fred Astaire . . . well, that was my mother."

RICK MORANIS, ELLEN GREENE

❧

Little Shop of Horrors, 1986
DIRECTOR: FRANK OZ
COSTUME DESIGNER: MARIT ALLEN

Seymour the Nerd and Audrey get married in much the same setting as that in *Tom, Dick and Harry.* Ellen Greene looks great until the man-eating plant decides to devour her, wedding gown and all. British costume designer Marit Allen said that when the plant devoured Audrey, "the lace tore beautifully and the tulle shredded perfectly." Here is pop culture paradise: Audrey looks like Barbie and Steve Martin, who plays a dentist, looks like Elvis. And, believe it or not, adorable Rick Moranis was considered by Stanley Kubrick for the lead in *Eyes Wide Shut* (1999).

VAN HEFLIN, KATHRYN GRAYSON

Seven Sweethearts, 1942
DIRECTOR: FRANK BORZAGE
COSTUME DESIGNER: HOWARD SHOUP

What a confusing ceremony! Seven sisters, including Kathryn Grayson and Marsha Hunt, all with boy's names, get married in Holland, the tulip capital of Michigan. They wear faux Dutch caps of lace trimmed with—what else—baby tulips!

DANNY KAYE, VIRGINIA MAYO

The Secret Life of Walter Mitty, 1947
DIRECTOR: NORMAN Z. MCLEOD
COSTUME DESIGNER: IRENE SHARAFF

Danny's a daydreamer who impersonates a ship's captain, a surgeon, an airline pilot, and a cowboy star, among others, and in every sequence, the dream girl of Technicolor films, Virginia Mayo, makes an appearance. Costume designer Sharaff has a field day with color for Mayo, using a Miami Beach palette to complement her good looks. Sharaff designed an over-the-top fashion show in Danny's "fashion designer dream"—interesting because producer Sam Goldwyn had previously fired her because she wasn't willing to design "simple" clothes.

JOAN FONTAINE, LAURENCE OLIVIER

❦

Rebecca, 1940

DIRECTOR: ALFRED HITCHCOCK

Rebecca was director Hitchcock's first American film and his only Oscar winner. At the time of casting, Olivier wanted his then girlfriend, Vivien Leigh, for the lead, and when Joan Fontaine got the part, he treated her poorly, making her feel insecure, which is exactly what Hitchcock wanted. Here, Joan and Olivier have just been married by a justice of the peace. The new Mrs. de Winter looks wistful when she spots the next bride, who is wearing a wedding gown and carrying flowers, so gallant Maxim buys her a bouquet from a nearby stand. After four very short marriages, Joan said, "Marriage, as an institution, is as dead as the dodo bird."

PAUL HENREID, KATHARINE HEPBURN

༄

Song of Love, 1947
DIRECTOR: CLARENCE BROWN
COSTUME DESIGNER: WALTER PLUNKETT

This film tells the story of the Schumanns and their good friend Johannes Brahms. Kate Hepburn plays Clara Wieck, the famed concert pianist, and must have practiced the piano diligently, as her fingerwork was more convincing than most actors'. Here is a very feminine Kate, sans pants, but it's the mid-nineteenth century and pantdressing didn't become popular until the 1940s. Pants would have come in handy after the wedding, when Kate and Paul trudge up five flights of steps to his flat, Kate still wearing her wedding gown.

DOROTHY MCGUIRE, GEORGE BRENT

❧

The Spiral Staircase, 1946
DIRECTOR: ROBERT SIODMAK
COSTUME DESIGNER: EDWARD STEVENSON

Dorothy McGuire made her Broadway debut as Martha Scott's understudy in *Our Town* in 1938 and David Selznick brought her to Hollywood five years later. In *The Spiral Staircase,* she plays the part of a mute who works as a maid in the home of George Brent. She is in love with a doctor and dreams about marrying him, but cannot say the words "I do." In her dream, the always dapper George Brent gives her away. George was a wedding expert; offscreen, he had six of them!

BURT LANCASTER, BARBARA STANWYCK

❧

Sorry, Wrong Number, 1948
DIRECTOR: ANATOLE LITVAK
COSTUME DESIGNER: EDITH HEAD

Barbara Stanwyck's *Sorry, Wrong Number* performance earned her a Best Actress nomination. This wedding portrait is displayed at Barbara's bedside, although the actual wedding is seen only in a flashback. In the movies, wedding and family portraits that are shown on-screen have to be costumed and shot only; there is no dialogue to learn. In the case of *A Perfect Murder* (1998), one sees the wedding portrait of Gwyneth Paltrow and Michael Douglas, but never the wedding. Before *The Lady Eve* (1941), Stanwyck was never a style setter, which was a prerequisite to stardom, but after Edith Head made her into a fashion plate in *Eve,* Barbara commanded bigger roles, more money, and Edith as her costume designer for every film.

ANN-MARGRET, ELVIS PRESLEY

Viva Las Vegas, 1964

DIRECTOR: GEORGE SIDNEY
COSTUME DESIGNER: DONFELD

Although the Elvis Presley movies were criticized for their lack of substance, they made over $150 million for their producers. The stars of *Viva Las Vegas* are Ann-Margret, Elvis, and racing cars; and, according to the costume designer, the wedding was a last-minute improv. But there were problems in Vegas. Elvis would keep A-M out until the early A.M., after which she would go directly to a 6:30 makeup call, looking exhausted. Elvis, on the other hand, didn't have to be in wardrobe until almost noon and, according to Donfeld, "he had Capricorn cheekbones, and it didn't matter how late he partied." Actually, they were *not* partying; they were driving all over town to the best hamburg joints!

TALIA SHIRE, SYLVESTER STALLONE

Rocky II, 1979

DIRECTOR: SYLVESTER STALLONE
COSTUME DESIGNERS: SANDRA BERKE
AND TOM BRONSON

Romance, Italian Stallion style! Rocky Balboa gets married in a large church with two attendants and no guests! Sly and Talia Shire are dressed in formal wedding attire when they walk home, where he takes off her headdress and veil, carries her to bed, still wearing her gown, and says, with great emotion, "You ain't ever gonna get rid of me."

CHARLES BRONSON, JILL IRELAND

❧

The Valachi Papers, 1972
DIRECTOR: TERENCE YOUNG
COSTUME DESIGNER: ANN ROTH

This movie was adapted from the Peter Maas novel about Joe Valachi, a Mafia informant, who was played by Charles Bronson. After years of B movies, tough-guy Bronson became a sex symbol in Europe at the age of fifty, known in France as *"le sacré monstre"* and in Italy as *"il brutto."* Jill Ireland, formerly a dancer, married Bronson in 1968 and appeared with him in over a dozen films until her untimely death in 1990. Costume designer Ann Roth was chosen by producer Dino De Laurentiis, who admired her work in *Midnight Cowboy* (1969) and gave her a member of Italy's royal family as her assistant.

JESSICA LANGE, ED HARRIS

❧

Sweet Dreams, 1985
DIRECTOR: KAREL REISZ
COSTUME DESIGNER: ANN ROTH

Jessica Lange, in her Oscar-nominated role as Patsy Cline, lip-synchs to Cline's country music and has great romantic moments with Ed Harris, who plays her husband. Jessica's costumes were influenced by Patsy's actual clothes. Costume designer Ann Roth was privy to the singer's wardrobe, designed by her mom, who also showed Ann her daughter's wedding hat, ensuring that the wedding ensemble for Jessica would look authentic.

RYAN O'NEAL, CYBILL SHEPHERD

❧

Chances Are, 1989
DIRECTOR: EMILE ARDOLINO
COSTUME DESIGNER: ALBERT WOLSKY

On Cybill's first wedding anniversary, she becomes a widow and, voilà, her husband, Ryan O'Neal, is reincarnated as a younger man, played by Robert Downey Jr., who can and does pull off the unexpected, acts his age, and, at the same time, turns "older woman" Cybill on. Some of Cybill's greatest moments have been on the small screen—remember Maddie in *Moonlighting*?—but her Albert Wolsky wedding gown of champagne stretch lace and chiffon is "big-screen glam."

DENNIS QUAID, WINONA RYDER

❧

Great Balls of Fire, 1989
DIRECTOR: JIM MCBRIDE
COSTUME DESIGNER: TRACY TYNAN

This is the story of the rise and fall of singer Jerry Lee Lewis, who said, "Well, if I'm going to hell, I'm going there playing the piano." Dennis Quaid is not really singing, but he is tickling the ivories as well as his thirteen-year-old cousin, played by Winona Ryder. She wears poodle skirts and ponytails and looks very casual at her wedding because it's just a stop on the way home from school. Winona is the real-life goddaughter of Timothy Leary, the LSD guru, and spent her childhood in a San Francisco commune.

SEAN YOUNG, MATT DILLON

❧

A Kiss Before Dying, 1991
DIRECTOR: JAMES DEARDEN
COSTUME DESIGNER:
MARIT ALLEN

Sean Young and Matt Dillon have an expensive formal wedding. Her earrings walked down the aisle before she did, quite the eighties look, but, according to designer Marit Allen, Sean's character was "a bit of a revolutionary." Her gown was designed by Catharine Walker, who also made many of the creations worn by Princess Diana.

BRUCE WILLIS, MICHELLE PFEIFFER

❧

The Story of Us, 1999
DIRECTOR: ROB REINER
COSTUME DESIGNER:
SHAY CUNLIFFE

In this dissection of a fifteen-year marriage, told in flashbacks, Michelle's good friend, played by Rita Wilson, says, "Marriage is the Jack Kevorkian of romance." How would she know? Rita has Tom Hanks!

HUGH GRANT, JEANNE TRIPPLEHORN

Mickey Blue Eyes, 1999
DIRECTOR: KELLY MAKIN
COSTUME DESIGNER: ELLEN MIROJNICK

Hugh Grant is an art exec working at a New York auction house and is in love with a mobster's daughter, played by Jeanne Tripplehorn. They have a beautiful church wedding and a great reception: all the crime families are there, and Hugh stages his own murder with the help of his father-in-law, James Caan. The FBI agents are among the wedding guests. Fuggedaboudit!

RUPERT EVERETT, MINNIE DRIVER

❧

An Ideal Husband, 1999
DIRECTOR: OLIVER PARKER
COSTUME DESIGNER:
CAROLINE HARRIS

Rupert Everett plays Lord Arthur Goring, a debonair, witty, and charming philanderer in Oscar Wilde's portrait of society. Rupert's career began in England during the early eighties, but it was his performance in *My Best Friend's Wedding* (1997) that made him an international sensation. The green carnation that he wears in his buttonhole is Arthur Goring's homage to Oscar Wilde, who, together with his circle of friends, wore one to suggest their sexual orientation.

MOLLY PARKER, RALPH FIENNES

✣

Sunshine, 2000
DIRECTOR: ISTVÁN SZABÓ
COSTUME DESIGNER:
GYÖRGYI SZAKÁCS

This is the story of the Sors family, three generations of central European Jews, and their life in Hungary. Ralph Fiennes plays the family patriarch; he also plays his son, who converts to Christianity, and his grandson, who is a Holocaust survivor returning to his roots. There are three weddings and many scenes in the Sors home, where the director lived as a child. Playing three roles is the only imaginable way Ralph Fiennes could top his performance in *The English Patient* (1996).

ANOTHER STATE OF *Matrimony*

PRIOR TO THE SIXTIES, HOLLYWOOD'S DEPICTION OF THE WEDDING WAS SACRED, ROMANTIC, TRADITIONAL, AND COSTUMED APPROPRIATELY FOR THE SERIOUSNESS OF THE OCCASION. BUT IN MORE RECENT FILMS, HOLLYWOOD'S TAKE ON THE WEDDING SCENE REFLECTS THE TIMES IN WHICH WE LIVE—ANYTHING AND EVERYTHING GOES. VENUES RANGING FROM BACKYARD BARBECUES TO UNDERWATER CEREMONIES, AS WELL AS ATTIRE FROM MILLION-DOLLAR GOWNS TO NUDITY WITH A VEIL, ARE NOW CONSIDERED ACCEPTABLE. EVEN MADISON AVENUE—WHICH AT ONE TIME REFLECTED BRIDAL BEAUTY IN MOSTLY COSMETIC ADS—NOW USES WEDDINGS IN NONTRADITIONAL SURROUNDINGS TO PROMOTE ALL TYPES OF CONSUMER PRODUCTS.

In the early movies, the wedding feast took a backseat to the extravagant costumes. But in today's films, the wedding food is often used as a point of comedy. For example, the *Goodbye Columbus* (1969) sweet table, complete with ice sculptures and enough food for an army, is a sight for hungry eyes and required a caterer as well as a food stylist. Both on and off the screen, hours of planning and decision making go into the wedding feast. Witness this scene from *True Love* (1989), starring Annabella Sciorra and Ron Eldard:

PLACE: A BANQUET HALL IN THE BRONX

CATERER: And what is your color scheme?

BRIDE: Rainbow . . . ya know . . . blue, green, yellow . . .

CATERER: You selected a menu of prime rib, baby peas, and mashed potatoes . . . We often color the mashed potatoes to match the color of the wedding . . . But, with rainbow, you can go with anything. Might I suggest pale blue?

BRIDE: Yah!

GROOM: Ged oudda heah. No, I'm not eatin' blue food!

BRIDE: What kind of blue?

CATERER: Sort of a sky blue.

BRIDE: It'll look cool.

GROOM: It'll look nutty . . . there's no such thing as blue food in real life.

CATERER: MICHAEL, THIS IS NOT REAL LIFE!

Previous page

ANNABELLA SCIORRA

❧

True Love, 1989

DIRECTOR: NANCY SAVOCA
COSTUME DESIGNER: DEBORAH ANDERKO

Nancy Savoca directed and cowrote *True Love,* a realistic comedy about an Italian wedding in the Bronx. The bride's and bridesmaids' dresses were influenced by Princess Diana's in that over-the-top eighties look. When the groom wants to go out drinking with his buddies after the reception, the heartbroken bride, played by Annabella Sciorra, finds solitude in only one place—until 2001, when she snuggles with Tony Soprano on HBO.

BUSTER KEATON

✦

Seven Chances, 1925
DIRECTOR: BUSTER KEATON

Buster is pursued by thousands of would-be brides. He has been left $7 million, providing he is married by 7 P.M. on his twenty-seventh birthday . . . which is that very day. When he proposes to his girlfriend, he explains that he must be married immediately—to anyone. She's insulted, of course, and turns down his offer. He then proposes to every woman he sees and even puts an ad in the newspaper. Exhausted by his failure, Keaton buys a bridal bouquet and goes to a church, just in case someone appears. A very young Jean Arthur is one of many to turn down Buster's proposal.

CHRIS O'DONNELL

✦

The Bachelor, 1999
DIRECTOR: GARY SINYOR
COSTUME DIRECTOR: TERRY DRESBACH

The Bachelor is the remake of the Buster Keaton classic *Seven Chances*. Costume designer Terry Dresbach had a problem: finding a thousand wedding gowns when her budget was $70 per gown. Miraculously, Terry found a wedding-gown collector in Massachusetts who, according to the collector's husband, "just couldn't stop buying them." They personally made the trip from Massachusetts to San Francisco with eight hundred gowns in a U-Haul. Just imagine those fittings! After a casting call, thousands of extras appeared, some wearing their own wedding gowns. But don't look too closely— some of those brides are guys in drag.

ELSA LANCHESTER, BORIS KARLOFF

ᴄ᷼ᴐ

The Bride of Frankenstein, 1935
DIRECTOR: JAMES WHALE

Ah, love in gloom! Unforgettable costumes, makeup, sets, and musical score highlight this sequel to the original *Frankenstein.* Elsa's monster tresses were inspired by Queen Nefertiti's hairdo. *The Bride of Frankenstein* was remade in 1985 as *The Bride,* with Sting playing the mad scientist.

WALTER MATTHAU, ELAINE MAY, RENEE TAYLOR

A New Leaf, 1971

DIRECTOR: ELAINE MAY
COSTUME DESIGNER: ANTHEA SYLBERT

When Walter Matthau learns that he is penniless, he decides to find a rich wife. Star/director/writer Elaine May was not pleased with the editing of her film (78 minutes were cut), but what remains is a sweet, hysterically funny film. The wedding and the wedding-night nightie have to be seen to be believed! Elaine, the star, couldn't figure out how to gracefully put on her nightgown, and suggested to designer Anthea Sylbert that they turn her difficulty into a comedy routine.

GINA LOLLOBRIGIDA, ROCK HUDSON

❧

Come September, 1961
DIRECTOR: ROBERT MULLIGAN
COSTUME DESIGNER: MORTON HAACK

Rock is a successful businessman who has a villa in Italy and a standby girlfriend, Gina Lollobridgida. He springs a surprise visit at the exact moment she is about to marry someone else. Gina appears in her wedding gown during most of the film, requiring dozens of copies to maintain its fresh appearance. The gown, firecracker headpiece, and veil never seem to get tired, although Gina tells Rock that she's tired—tired of being the "girl of the month."

WEDDING OF ROCK HUDSON
AND PHYLLIS GATES, 1955

The tall (six foot six inches) and great-looking Rock Hudson was an Oscar
nominee for *Giant* (1956), and also won *Look* magazine's Star of the Year award.
For three years, he was married to his agent's secretary, an attempt by Hollywood
to discourage rumors of his homosexuality. In 1985, Hudson was the first major
public figure to die of AIDS. Elizabeth Taylor created the American Foundation for
AIDS Research (AMFAR) in memory of Rock Hudson, her dear friend.

SIMONETTA STEPANELLI

❧

The Godfather, 1972
DIRECTOR: FRANCIS FORD COPPOLA
COSTUME DESIGNER: ANNA HILL JOHNSTONE

"In Sicily, women are more dangerous than shotguns," Michael Corleone
(Al Pacino) is advised when he first spots the beautiful Apollonia (Simonetta
Stepanelli). During their wedding, Michael, a Mafia don's son who is hiding out
in Sicily, the bride, and the wedding guests are heavily guarded. Warren Beatty,
Jack Nicholson, and Dustin Hoffman all turned down Pacino's part. *The
Godfather* won Oscars for Best Actor (rejected by Marlon Brando), Best
Picture, Best Director, and Best Costume.

TIA CARRERE

Hollow Point, 1995

DIRECTOR: SIDNEY J. FURIE
COSTUME DESIGNER:
NICOLETTA MASSONE

Tia Carrere plays an FBI agent willing to spoil her own wedding to bring down the bad guy. Hawaii-born Tia was offered a role on *Baywatch,* but turned it down to audition for *Wayne's World* (1992). She originally appeared on TV's *General Hospital* as Nurse Chung in the eighties.

SHEMAR MOORE, SUSAN DALIAN

The Brothers, 2001

DIRECTOR: GARY HARDWICK
COSTUME DESIGNER: DEBRAE LITTLE

Instead of saying "I do," Moore (TV's *The Young and the Restless*) leaves a message on Susan's voice mail saying, "I don't." Susan does what any jilted bride dreams of doing and brings her man to his senses, using a shotgun for persuasion. Very married writer/director Gary Hardwick said, "The story came about from my life *before* I got married. Each guy is supposed to be one side of my twisted personality." The groom-to-be and his friends get physical on the basketball court, giving the guys the chance to be "partially undressed for our female audience," laughed Hardwick.

BARBRA STREISAND

Funny Girl, 1968

DIRECTOR: WILLIAM WYLER

COSTUME DESIGNER: IRENE SHARAFF

"Hello, Gorgeous!" Barbra's Oscar-winning screen debut is the life story of comedienne Fanny Brice, the first Jewish heroine in the talkies to speak with a Lower East Side accent. Florenz Ziegfeld informs Fanny that she had to play this scene in the *Follies* straight, no joking around. Fanny refuses and puts a pillow in her gown for the wedding scene. In the early part of the twentieth century, during the height of the *Ziegfeld Follies,* seeing a very pregnant bride was definitely unheard of. Nowadays, maternity wedding gowns are readily available.

JOHN SAVAGE, BEVERLY D'ANGELO

Hair, 1979

DIRECTOR: MILOS FORMAN
COSTUME DESIGNER: ANN ROTH

John Savage arrives in New York City from Oklahoma and befriends a group of hippies as he is about to leave for Vietnam. His wedding fantasy is induced by drugs: he is marrying Beverly D'Angelo, who wears a gorgeous crocheted gown and doesn't stand in profile until the conclusion of the sequence. John comes down quickly! According to designer Ann Roth, Milos Forman gave birth to the pregnancy, which did not happen in the Broadway musical. Beverly and Al Pacino became the parents of twins in 2001.

KATHARINE ROSS, DUSTIN HOFFMAN

❧

The Graduate, 1967
DIRECTOR: MIKE NICHOLS
COSTUME DESIGNER: PATRICIA ZIPPRODT

College graduate Hoffman is having an affair with his parents' friend, the seductive Anne Bancroft, who in real life is actually only a few years his senior. The scene stealers are Paul Simon and Art Garfunkel, who wrote the unforgettable music, and also Buck Henry, who wrote the script. Robert Redford turned down Hoffman's part and director Nichols won the Oscar. Katharine Ross, playing Bancroft's daughter, won the guy.

ANNETTE O'TOOLE

<svg>✂</svg>

Foolin' Around, 1980

DIRECTOR: RICHARD T. HEFFRON
COSTUME DESIGNER: JOE TOMPKINS

This is a fifties-type comedy about a nerd who is chasing a rich, engaged girl. *Foolin' Around* has an overly exaggerated *Graduate*-type ending with Gary Busey racing to rescue the unhappy bride, Annette O'Toole. When she bolts, her mom, played by Cloris Leachman, says, "Distinguished guests and stockholders, do I have a surprise for you," and proceeds to don her daughter's discarded veil and marry the old codger, Tony Randall.

KIM BASINGER, DAN AYKROYD

❧

My Stepmother Is an Alien, 1988
DIRECTOR: RICHARD BENJAMIN
COSTUME DESIGNER: AGGIE GUERARD RODGERS

Kim Basinger is an alien who wants to make contact with a nerdy scientist, played by Dan Aykroyd, to save her planet from destruction. Along the way, she falls in human love and gets married in a sweet, conservative-looking gown—from the front, that is. Costume designer Aggie Rodgers asked Kim what she thought an alien might wear, and Kim suggested a heart-shaped, cutout back, surrounded by baby jewels. Basinger kept her *L.A. Confidential* costumes; one wonders if she also kept this gown and wore it when she married Alec Baldwin in 1993.

DEBRA WINGER

❦

Terms of Endearment, 1983
DIRECTOR: JAMES BROOKS
COSTUME DESIGNER: KRISTI ZEA

Is Debra Winger depressed because she turns in a splendid, tear-jerking performance and everyone else got an Oscar? We watch her character grow up; marry her sweetheart, Flap, played convincingly by Jeff Daniels; and have lots of babies, an affair, and a great deathbed scene. Only Shirley MacLaine and Jack Nicholson's assignation scene tops all of that.

CAMERON DIAZ

❧

Feeling Minnesota, 1996
DIRECTOR: STEVEN BAIGELMAN
COSTUME DESIGNER: EUGENIE BAFALOUKOS

The movie begins with Cameron Diaz, a former stripper, wearing a distressed wedding gown, running down the railroad tracks. She has a backyard wedding, complete with a gross bridegroom, played by Vincent D'Onofrio, whom she doesn't love. Maybe it's because of his outfit: powder blue polyester with a ruffled shirt and the jacket split open down the back. There is even a powder blue wedding cake. In 2000, Cameron's wedding gown, in the condition seen on the screen, was for sale for $850, together with a picture of Diaz wearing the dress before the distressing occurred.

"*In the first half of my life, I was best known as Florenz Ziegfeld's wife. In the second half, they remember me not as the great Ziegfeld's widow, but as Glinda the Good Witch.*"

—Billie Burke

NICOLAS CAGE, SARAH JESSICA PARKER

Honeymoon in Vegas, 1992
DIRECTOR: ANDREW BERGMAN
COSTUME DESIGNER: JULIE WEISS

This movie is from the comedy screenwriter who gave us *Soapdish, Fletch, The In-Laws,* and *Blazing Saddles:* Andrew Bergman. The plot is the same as *Indecent Proposal* (1993), but with a lot more fun: Elvis Presley music, and as wedding attendants, the Flying Elvises. Designer Julie Weiss commented, "Imagine anyone taking attention away from Elvis impersonators." It must have been the bridal G-string. What could be better? Only Sarah Jessica's real wedding. When she married Matthew Broderick in 1997, she wore black, but kept her fans in the dark regarding the details, unlike her TV character, Carrie Bradshaw (*Sex and the City*), who tells all.

MARISA TOMEI, ROBERT DOWNEY JR.

Chaplin, 1992
DIRECTOR:
RICHARD ATTENBOROUGH
COSTUME DESIGNERS:
ELLEN MIROJNICK AND JOHN MOLLO

Chaplin chronicles the life and loves of filmmaker Charlie Chaplin, who said, "If you want to understand me, watch my movies." Playing "the Little Tramp" for the very first time, Chaplin, brilliantly portrayed by Robert Downey Jr., interrupts a silent-film wedding, trying to lure the bride's love and get rid of the groom—in front of the camera, of course. The silent film being shot starred Mabel Normand (Marisa Tomei), who was then the queen of comedy.

NANCY TRAVIS, MIKE MYERS

So I Married an Axe Murderer, 1993
DIRECTOR: THOMAS SCHLAMME
COSTUME DESIGNER: KIMBERLY A. TILLMAN

Mike Myers plays a bachelor and the character's own father, a funny Scotsman. When he finally gets married, he wears red argyles, kilts, and a sporran, the purselike pouch that holds down the front of the kilt. Designer Kimberly Tillman said that Mike actually wore the "Mackenzie" plaid, which was his name in the film. But Kimberly had a problem: the Highland Society of Scotland had not sent enough kilts for both characters, so she had to find a Scottish tailor to stretch (i.e., to get more out of less) and, at the same time, match the plaid. Mike really got into kilt dressing, except for the tighty whities that he wore underneath it all. When kilted Guy Ritchie married Madonna in December 2000, Kim helped with her knowledge of the subject.

CHRISTINA RICCI, RAUL JULIA, ANJELICA HUSTON, JOAN CUSACK, STRUYCKEN CAREL, CHRISTOPHER LLOYD

❧

Addams Family Values, 1993
DIRECTOR: BARRY SONNENFELD
COSTUME DESIGNER: THEONI V. ALDREDGE

Joan Cusack appears as Debbie, "the nanny from the agency," wearing a blond wig and a white Lycra spandex uniform. She says to Morticia, played by Anjelica Huston, "I love your dress . . . it's so tight." Costume designer Theoni Aldredge recalls that when Anjelica tried on her Morticia costume, she thanked her for allowing her room to sit and to go to the bathroom, unlike her original *Addams Family* (1991) costume. Joan plots to marry Uncle Fester for his money; when saying her wedding vows, she starts rehearsing widowhood! While waiting for Fester to expire, as per her plan, Joan is in a bar where the customers are singing "Macho Man," the same song that does in her marriage to Kevin Kline in the film *In & Out* (1997).

WEDDING OF ANJELICA HUSTON AND ROBERT GRAHAM, MAY 23, 1992

࿎

Anjelica Huston, wearing a Giorgio Armani white suit, married renowned sculptor Robert Graham at the Beverly Hills Hotel. Anjelica, who modeled for Norman Norell in the early seventies, is an actress, a director, and an Oscar winner (*Prizzi's Honor,* 1985). Her wedding reception took place on a tented lot that is now Anjelica and Robert's home, in Venice, California. Collaborating with designer Richard Tyler, she designed a white taffeta flamenco dress with a pearl-beaded jacket for the party.

WE ARE *Family*

*W*hen a bride gets married, she gets more than just a husband—she gets a family, for better or for worse. And it's no different in Hollywood. In 1927, Joan Crawford, discussing Norma Shearer's relationship with Norma's future mother-in-law, said, "Irving Thalberg — he was a mama's boy if ever there was one."

Irving's poor health made his mother, Henrietta, sick with worry. She always had a warm meal ready for him, made him stay in bed when he was pale, and waited on him hand and foot. Although Irving left his position with Carl Laemmle, the head of Universal Studios, not wanting to marry his daughter, it was Rosabelle Laemmle who didn't want to take a chance on becoming a young widow. Irving's new boss, Louis B. Mayer, discouraged both of his daughters from any romantic interest in Thalberg. When Mrs. Thalberg met Norma Shearer, she was impressed; when Norma converted to Judaism, her mother-in-law blessed the marriage.

After their honeymoon, the newlywed Thalbergs moved in with the senior Thalbergs, where they remained until four years later, when Norma became pregnant. While they were living with Irving's parents, Henrietta relieved Norma of all household duties so she could concentrate on her career. Norma was the "perfect wife": she made it clear that Irving was the star of their marriage and his mother was the star of their home!

Marilyn Monroe found in her relationship with Arthur Miller's parents the warm and loving family life that she missed as a child. She immediately called Isadore and Augusta Miller "Dad" and "Mom."

During their engagement, Arthur said: "Until recently, I took my family for granted. But Marilyn never had one, and she made me appreciate what that means. When you see how much a family matters to her and you understand the depth of that feeling, you'd have to be an ox not to respond."

Warm and loving is not the family feeling that Gene Tierney described about her June 1941 wedding to designer Oleg Cassini. In her autobiography, she said:

> Oleg and I had bought tickets for that Sunday on a commercial flight to Las Vegas. So as not to arouse my mother's suspicions, I left the house dressed casually in a blouse and skirt, and told her I was going on a picnic. . . . For his disguise, Oleg dressed like an American businessman, or rather, his idea of one. He looked about as much like a businessman as I did, dressed in a polo coat and a felt hat and carrying a briefcase.

When they reached Las Vegas, they were driven to the home of a justice of the peace to say their vows. Afterward, she called her mother. Gene wrote: "When she answered, my voice sang with excitement: 'Mother, dear, you've got the most wonderful son-in-law . . .' 'Where are you?' she asked. 'I'm in Las Vegas, and Oleg and I have just been married.' 'You can keep him,' she said. Before I could get out another word, I heard the phone click."

At one time, the world's problems seemed minuscule compared to the making of a wedding. Many letters to advice columnists are about that very subject: whom to invite; whom not to invite; what Mom wants the bride to wear and what Dad is willing and able to spend; and the in-laws—making family relationships even more strained than usual.

But on that day, at that magic moment, the photographer always captures a beautiful scene: the bridal couple, surrounded by their loved ones, smiling happily and looking like the trials and tribulations of their wedding planning never occurred.

Previous page

MARLON BRANDO AND FAMILY

❧

The Godfather, 1972
DIRECTOR: FRANCIS FORD COPPOLA
COSTUME DESIGNER: ANNA HILL JOHNSTONE

This is not your typical backyard wedding; it's at a Mafia don's estate with a cast of thousands and uninvited FBI agents checking license plates. Nothing, not even a daughter's wedding, interrupts the "family business."

FRANK MORGAN, JOAN CRAWFORD

I Live My Life, 1935

DIRECTOR: W. S. VAN DYKE
COSTUME DESIGNER: ADRIAN

Joan Crawford plays a bored society girl who goes to Greece, where she meets Brian Aherne and falls in love. He follows her back to New York, but doesn't care for her lifestyle, which includes lots of Adrian-designed dresses, most with oversize collars, making smoking impossible for undersized Joan. For the aisle walk, Adrian added two accessories to his classic wedding gown: a Bo Peep doily on Joan's head and a satin cape trimmed with an entire field of flowers. Crawford had five husbands, including Douglas Fairbanks Jr. and Franchot Tone. Each one of the marriages lasted four years, except the first, which lasted only one. Bette Davis said of Crawford: "She slept with every male star at MGM except Lassie."

CHARLES WINNINGER, IRENE DUNNE

Showboat, 1936

DIRECTOR: JAMES WHALE
COSTUME DESIGNER: VERA WEST

Irene Dunne was the daughter of a steamship inspector and became a leading lady of the musical stage, appearing as Nola in the road company of *Showboat* in 1929. Her film dad, Charles Winninger, was the original "Captain Andy" on the stage in 1927. The only thing missing from this version (the story was also filmed in 1929 and 1951) was Technicolor. With Paul Robeson, Helen Morgan, "Queenie," and "Rochester," who could ask for more?

BARBARA STANWYCK

Stella Dallas, 1937

DIRECTOR: KING VIDOR
COSTUME DESIGNER: OMAR KIAM

Barbara Stanwyck insisted that this was the best acting work she had ever done, and also the best film she ever appeared in. She was only thirty at the time, and had to be aged considerably during the film, as did Bette Midler during the remake, *Stella,* in 1990. The wedding scene is especially poignant (about a five-hankie rating). Barbara stands outside, in a torrential downpour, watching the daughter she has given up get married.

HENRY FONDA, BARBARA STANWYCK

❦

The Lady Eve, 1941
DIRECTOR: PRESTON STURGES
COSTUME DESIGNER: EDITH HEAD

In this film, Fonda plays a young, adorable, and rich ophiologist—a scientist specializing in reptiles! And, speaking of snakes, Barbara and her screen dad, Charles Coburn, play card sharks on the prowl for their next victim. Enter Henry Fonda—and making an even greater entrance, Edith Head's great costumes for Stanwyck, a forties look that was copied by every manufacturer and worn by every woman, including Kim Basinger in *L.A. Confidental* (1997). On her wedding night, Stanwyck wears not only her publicity-shot negligee, but also a snood, a fancy hairnet made popular by Adrian for Hedy Lamarr in *I Take This Woman* (1939).

ELIZABETH TAYLOR, SPENCER TRACY

❧

Father of the Bride, 1950
DIRECTOR: VINCENTE MINNELLI
COSTUME DESIGNERS: HELEN ROSE
AND WALTER PLUNKETT

There were two costume designers on this film, Helen Rose for the women and Walter Plunkett for the men. It wasn't until 1969 during the making of *Butch Cassidy and the Sundance Kid* that a woman designer, Edith Head, was allowed to dress both the men and the women. But the reverse was always possible. Vera West, wardrobe head of Universal, said, "It takes a woman to understand how to dress women." The premiere of this film was delayed until two days after the real wedding of star Liz Taylor to Nicky Hilton, so there could be maximum marketing of the movie.

KIMBERLY WILLIAMS, STEVE MARTIN

❧

Father of the Bride, 1991
DIRECTOR: CHARLES SHYER
COSTUME DESIGNER: SUSAN BECKER

How do you remake a classic? You use Steve Martin in the lead, together with Martin Short and B. D. Wong as the wedding planners—and a snowstorm in California and melting swans. When Steve decides to save some money by wearing his old tux, he bursts out of it while modeling for the family. Designer Susan Becker had it rigged so it would rip straight up the back and the "rrrrrrrrrip" sound was done by the audio person. On the big day, when Steve sees his wife, played by Diane Keaton, all dressed for the wedding, he says, "You shouldn't have looked this beautiful. It's not fair to the bride." There are tears in his voice—and in the eyes of every woman watching this film.

LARAINE DAY

❧

The Locket, 1946
DIRECTOR: JOHN BRAHM
COSTUME DESIGNER: MICHAEL WOULFE

Laraine is about to marry Gene Raymond and is receiving some last-minute instructions from her future mother-in-law when Brian Aherne appears and says she is a liar, a kleptomaniac, and worse. Laraine asked the studio to hire designer Michael Woulfe because she fell in love with the costumes he designed for Sylvia Sidney in *Blood on the Sun* (1945). Years later, when Laraine asked him to design her wardrobe for the remake of *Alice Adams* (1935), Woulfe said, "Don't redo it, for heaven's sake, just re-release the original. Hepburn was great." The studio took his advice.

OLIVIA DE HAVILLAND, YVETTE MIMIEUX

❧

Light in the Piazza, 1962
DIRECTOR: GUY GREEN
COSTUME DESIGNER: DIOR

Yvette is a mentally challenged young woman who goes to Italy with her mom and meets George Hamilton, who falls madly in love with her. Imagine George with an Italian accent! And just imagine the Dior wardrobe for Olivia de Havilland. Ms. de Havilland kept the Diors and, in the nineties, sold them at a London auction. The successful bidder was the House of Dior, adding to their collection.

JOEL MCCREA, CLAUDETTE COLBERT, RUDY VALLEE, MARY ASTOR

The Palm Beach Story, 1942

DIRECTOR: PRESTON STURGES
COSTUME DESIGNER: IRENE

Another really screwy Sturges comedy—but that's what America needed in 1942. Because Claudette has lost her suitcase, millionaire Rudy (John D. Hackensacker III) takes her shopping for what he hoped would eventually be her trousseau. The bill reads:

12 pairs of stockings	$19.98	3 fancy brassieres	$24.00
12 pairs of shoes	100.00	3 girdles	30.00
8 handbags	212.00	2 breakfasts	1.50
6 slips	96.00	Gorgeous dinner gown (with sequins)	212.00
8 hats	146.00	1 dress	165.00
Perfume	196.00	1 dress	69.00
24 hankies	36.00	1 dress	290.00
1 dozen fancy pants	60.00	Coat	285.00

When Rudy asks Claudette if she needs a bracelet for the dress with the bracelet sleeves, he buys her a big diamond one. Only the wedding can top the shopping spree: Rudy marries Colbert's identical twin and Joel McCrea's identical twin marries Mary Astor—and that all happens in the last ten seconds of the movie!

WEDDING OF EDDIE FISHER
AND DEBBIE REYNOLDS,
SEPTEMBER 26, 1955

Debbie Reynolds and Eddie Fisher were married at Grossinger's Resort in New York's Catskill Mountains. Nineteen days later, Mike Todd, Eddie's best friend, threw them a party that was cohosted by gossip columnist Louella Parsons. The following year, America's Sweethearts appeared in *Bundle of Joy,* their only film together. In the movie, they lived happily ever after.

FRED ASTAIRE, DEBBIE REYNOLDS,
TAB HUNTER, LILLI PALMER

The Pleasure of His Company, 1961
DIRECTOR: GEORGE SEATON
COSTUME DESIGNER: EDITH HEAD

Fred Astaire, playing an egomaniacal bon vivant, arrives from Kenya just in time to upset his estranged daughter's (Debbie Reynolds) wedding plans. He hounds his ex's new husband, and tries to persuade his daughter to travel with him, see the world, and dump her betrothed, Tab Hunter. But the star of the film is costume designer Edith Head, who makes a cameo appearance as the bridal-shop designer at Magnin's in San Francisco. As she is helping Debbie during a fitting, she has a spoken line: "Be careful of the net overskirt—don't let it touch the floor." Edith's advice was given weekly on TV's *House Party* in the fifties.

PENNY PEYSER, ALAN ARKIN, PETER FALK

The In-Laws, 1979

DIRECTOR: ARTHUR HILLER
COSTUME DESIGNER: PHYLLIS GARR

This is a moment of insanity with Peter Falk, who plays a faux FBI agent/father of the groom; and Alan Arkin, who is Sheldon Kornpett, a nice, ordinary dentist/ father of the bride; and Richard Libertini, playing General Garcia, a Latin American dictator who thinks he is Señor Wences, a ventriloquist who appeared on *The Ed Sullivan Show* in the fifties. *What a trip*– and what an entrance to their children's wedding: dropping out of a helicopter, wearing top hats and tails and bearing a wedding check for a million dollars. If the bride only knew about the million, she would have bought a nicer gown!

CAROL BURNETT, PAUL DOOLEY, MIA FARROW, DENNIS CHRISTOPHER, AMY STRYCKER

A Wedding, 1978

DIRECTOR: ROBERT ALTMAN
COSTUME DESIGNER:
J. ALLEN HIGHFILL

There is nothing exceptional about this wedding, except the dead grandma in the upstairs bedroom, played by Lillian Gish in her one hundredth movie, and Carol Burnett, without her Bob Mackie dress, and Geraldine Chaplin, the lesbian party planner in flowered chiffon, and Mia Farrow, the unmarried pregnant sister, and Amy Stryker, the bride with braces, and Viveca Lindfors and Howard Duff as drunken guests. *Oy vey;* it's just like a real wedding!!!

MADELINE KAHN, MOLLY RINGWALD, ALAN ALDA

Betsy's Wedding, 1990
DIRECTOR: ALAN ALDA
COSTUME DESIGNER: MARY MALIN

Mother always knows best—or does she? Not if it's Betsy's wedding. Molly Ringwald used to look pretty in pink, but she leaves that to her sis, Ally Sheedy, the policeperson. At the last second, Betsy makes some funky alterations to her gown. They should have also made alterations on the leaky tent; when it starts to pour, everyone takes off their shoes and has a perfectly ducky time.

JOANNE WOODWARD, MARGARET WELSH

Mr. & Mrs. Bridge, 1990
DIRECTOR: JAMES IVORY
COSTUME DESIGNER:
CAROL RAMSEY

This film focuses on a straitlaced Kansas City family during the thirties and forties. Paul Newman and Joanne Woodward are wonderful, as usual, and Joan's mother-of-the-bride ensemble matches her husband's "baby blues." When asked about his marriage, Paul said, "Why fool around with hamburger when you have steak at home?" Steak, and salad dressing and popcorn, no doubt.

PAULA MARSHALL, DENNIS FARINA

❧

That Old Feeling, 1997
DIRECTOR: CARL REINER
COSTUME DESIGNER:
ROBERT DE MORA

Divorced parents Dennis Farina and Bette Midler fall back in lust at their daughter's wedding. Later, when the bride and groom are in their hotel room, coincidentally next to the room Mom and Dad have taken, the bride says, "I'm not going to stay here and listen to my parents having sex on my wedding night."

DENNIS FARINA, BETTE MIDLER

❧

That Old Feeling, 1997
DIRECTOR: CARL REINER
COSTUME DESIGNER: ROBERT DE MORA

Designer Bob De Mora didn't want Bette to wear a mother-of-the-bride color because, in the film, she's a flamboyant actress and needs to upstage everyone, including her daughter. Bette's red gown stands out and then some, because Bob dressed all the female guests in pastels. Dennis Farina's wife wears a $1,500 designer hat, which somehow was forgotten in the church scene but suddenly appears on her head at the garden reception. In 1984, the Divine Miss M. was married to Martin von Haselberg by a Las Vegas minister impersonating Elvis.

DREW BARRYMORE, CHRISTINA PICKLES

❧

The Wedding Singer, 1998
DIRECTOR: FRANK CORACI
COSTUME DESIGNER: MONA MAY

Drew has fallen for Adam Sandler and knows that marrying her fiancé is a big mistake, but she takes Adam as a friend to a meeting with her wedding planner. The planner, thinking that Adam and Drew are a couple, says, "I can tell you'll stay together forever . . . like Donald and Ivana, Woody and Mia, and Burt and Loni." In this scene, designer Mona May keeps Drew's wedding gown simple and classic, because her character "was not about stuff." Mona wanted the audience to concentrate on Drew's predicament: how to get out of her forthcoming marriage, rather than just ogling the wedding gown.

DREW BARRYMORE

❧

The Wedding Singer, 1998
DIRECTOR: FRANK CORACI
COSTUME DESIGNER: MONA MAY

This cult movie was written by Tim Herlihy, Adam Sandler's college roommate, with a little help from Adam and Carrie Fisher. Sweet and sincere, Drew Barrymore (the granddaughter of John) is engaged to a total jerk and works as a waitress doing weddings and bar mitzvahs—where Adam Sandler is the wedding and bar mitzvah singer.

BILL HUNTER, TONI COLLETTE

Muriel's Wedding, 1994
DIRECTOR: P. J. HOGAN
COSTUME DESIGNER: TERRY RYAN

When Muriel catches the bridal bouquet at a wedding, the girls say, "Give it back, Muriel. You'll never get married." So she sets out to prove them wrong. She changes cities and friends, visits bridal salons, trying on gowns, and saves the Polaroids in an album. Muriel is paid to marry a professional swimmer, who needs a wife to stay in Australia and compete. No bride has ever been as radiant on that walk down the aisle!

MILI AVITAL, LENA OLIN, CLAIRE DANES

Polish Wedding, 1998
DIRECTOR: THERESA CONNELLY
COSTUME DESIGNER: DONNA ZAKOWSKA

Marc Chagall's painting of *The Betrothed* was the costume designer's inspiration for the wedding gown Claire Danes wears, which is very decorative and a complete contrast to the barren Kowalski-land of Detroit's Hamtramack. The entire film was shot in the very neighborhood of Hamtramack where the director grew up, the second largest Polish community in America. Lots of fun, borscht, and kielbasa were had by all! But how can the bride be the star of her own wedding when her mom is played by the beautiful and sensuous Lena Olin?

JANET JACKSON, EDDIE MURPHY

><

Nutty Professor II: The Klumps, 2000
DIRECTOR: PETER SEGAL
COSTUME DESIGNER: SHAREN DAVIS

Janet Jackson told designer Sharen Davis that her favorite costume—ever—was *The Klumps'* wedding gown because she had never worn one. It was made from two size-20 gowns (her mom-in-law, one of the many roles played by Eddie Murphy, was generous in both girth and giving). After the wrap, Janet's nine-year secret marriage to Rene Elizondo was disclosed—when he filed for divorce.

TOM SKERRITT, DIANE KEATON, JULIETTE LEWIS

The Other Sister, 1999

DIRECTOR: GARRY MARSHALL
COSTUME DESIGNER: GARY JONES

Pasadena is the home of the Rose Bowl and also enormous roses. According to costume designer Gary Jones, when the roses arrived for the wedding scene, they were so big that they completely covered the bodies of the bridesmaids, and the single-rose boutonnieres for the men were each as big as a head of cabbage. Gary had to perform last-minute pruning. At the end of the movie, when Juliette Lewis gets married, it rained for three days straight, but director Garry Marshall found that patience paid off. There was a small break in the weather, allowing the marching band to come down the street, playing the bridal couple's song: "76 Trombones."

RICHARD GERE, KATE HUDSON

꒰꒱

Dr. T and the Women, 2000

DIRECTOR: ROBERT ALTMAN

COSTUME DESIGNER: DONA GRANATA

Coordinating the bridal party with the weather was a great opportunity for designer Dona Granata, who loves to work with director Robert Altman because "he is such a great visualist." With a storm brewing, and an outdoor wedding in the works, what better color to use than a sky-blue gray for the father of the bride, Richard Gere, and his screen daughter, Goldie Hawn's talented real-life daughter, Kate Hudson? Dona selected blue gray cashmere for Gere's morning coat, which was then made up in Italy by Brioni. Kate wore layers of tulle, graduating from white to blue gray and topped with Harry Winston diamonds. It was a beautiful storm! Kate had such fun that she did it again. In December, she married rocker Chris Robinson at Goldie Hawn and Kurt Russell's Colorado home.

Private Lives

On hearing about Gloria Swanson's fifth marriage, her first husband, Wallace Beery, said, "Damned if she didn't keep on getting married! I got her into an awful bad habit."

At one time, the phrase "private lives" would refer to the Noel Coward play or to a popular column in *Life* magazine. But in the year 2002, there is nothing private about celebrities' lives. When you hear the words "movie-star wedding," what immediately comes to mind is millions of dollars, designer dresses that cost thousands, and how long the marriage will last. In 1936, the divorce rate in Hollywood was four times the national average. And today, not only does the public copy the fashion worn by the stars, but the stars' divorce rates as well. In 1994, there were 1.2 million American divorces—three times the 1960 figure.

Elizabeth Taylor, like many Hollywood stars, has been married and married and married . . .

1. Elizabeth Taylor's marriage to Nicky Hilton coincided with the release of *Father of the Bride* (1950). In preparation for the wedding, Liz and her mom went shopping at Marshall Field's in Chicago, buying silver flatware, Limoges china, Swedish crystal, and Italian lace-trimmed sheets. Her future father-in-law gave her a block of Hilton stock and an all-expenses-paid three-month honeymoon in Europe. Helen Rose designed the wedding gown, a gift from MGM. It was a creation of white satin embroidered with beads and seed pearls and took two months to complete. With it, Liz wore a tiara and ten yards

of veiling. Sydney Guilaroff, MGM's hairstylist, overheard Liz arguing with her mom about her refusal to wear stockings under her gown.

At the church, prominent pews were assigned to the William Powells, Phil Harris and Alice Faye, the Gene Kellys, the Bing Crosbys, the Walter Pidgeons, Dick Powell and June Allyson, the Red Skeltons, the Van Johnsons, Margaret O'Brien, and Roddy McDowall. May 6, 1950, was one of the hottest days of the year, with temperatures over a hundred degrees. Although Roman Catholic ceremonies at that time did not allow a kiss, the monsignor was swept away with the glamour of the moment and gave his permission. Seven hundred guests went through the receiving line at the Bel Air Country Club to have a piece of the five-tier, vanilla-frosted wedding cake. Liz wore an Edith Head ensemble as her "going-away suit."

2. Liz and Michael Wilding entertained a handful of their friends in the honeymoon suite of the Berkeley Hotel in London. They ate broiled lobster, roast duck, and poached salmon. And then, four days later, on February 21, 1952, Liz married her second husband, wearing a gray wool suit with a rolled collar and cuffs of white organdy designed by Helen Rose. At midnight, they ordered a room-service dinner, consisting of split pea soup, bacon and eggs, chocolate mousse, and champagne.

3. Liz and Mike Todd got married on February 2, 1957, in Acapulco. She was two months pregnant with Todd's baby. Eddie Fisher and Debbie Reynolds were the best man and the matron of honor. Helen Rose designed a deep-blue cocktail dress for the wedding. The ceremony was held at the villa of former Mexican president Miguel Alemán, followed by an outdoor reception. Guests ate caviar, oversize prawns, lobster tails, and spit-roasted pig, accompanied by champagne. Mexican screen legend Cantinflas's wedding gift to the couple was a fireworks display.

4. Liz and Eddie Fisher married on May 12, 1959, in Las Vegas's Temple Beth Shalom. Liz's children were there, and Mike Todd Jr. was the best man. Eddie wore a yarmulke and a blue suit, and Liz had on a Jean Louis green chiffon dress with a softly draped hood. The bride and groom stood underneath a *chuppah* and recited their vows in Hebrew. Liz said, "I've never been happier in my life."

5. On March 15, 1964, Liz and Richard Burton got married in Montreal, in a suite at the Ritz Carlton. Irene Sharaff designed a replica of the yellow gown Liz wore in the first scene of *Cleopatra* (1962). She wore white hyacinths in her hair and the gift she received from Richard for her thirty-second birthday: diamond-and-emerald earrings.

6. Burton proposed again. It was after Liz left a note under his pillow that read in part: "Maybe I'll carry you off on a white charger, but I'd prefer it to be the other way round." The ceremony took place on October 10, 1975, in Botswana, on the edge of a riverbank. Liz wore a long green robe embroidered with exotic birds; Richard was in white slacks and a red turtleneck. He gave her another diamond, adding to her huge collection. She said, "We'll be together, always."

7. On December 4, 1976, Liz and Senator John Warner got married on top of Engagement Hill at the senator's farm, where he had proposed and a herd of his cattle had just deposited some unwelcome wedding gifts. Liz wore a dress of lavender gray, with gray suede boots and a coat of silver fox. She had on a matching turban and carried a bouquet of heather. They had an Episcopal ceremony and honeymooned in Israel.

8. On October 5, 1990, Liz and Larry Fortensky were married at Michael Jackson's Neverland Ranch with 150 guests in attendance, including the Ronald Reagans and the Gerald Fords. The bride and groom met at the Betty Ford Clinic for alcohol dependency and drug addiction. Liz wore a $25,000 lemon yellow wedding gown, a gift from designer Valentino. Her hairdresser, Jose Eber, was the best man and Michael Jackson paid for the $1.5 million wedding.

Previous page

WEDDING OF NICKY HILTON AND ELIZABETH TAYLOR, MAY 6, 1950

Liz's favorite wedding gifts were from her family: a Hals painting and a mink coat from Dad, and a white mink stole from Mom. Don Taylor, the *Father of the Bride* groom, received a postcard from the honeymooning Mrs. Hilton that read, "Movies are better than ever—but honeymoon is better than Movie!"

RUDOLPH VALENTINO, POLA NEGRI, MAE MURRAY, COUNT DAVID MDIVANI

❧

WEDDING OF MAE MURRAY AND COUNT DAVID MDIVANI, 1926

Mae Murray was married to Count David Mdivani for seven years. In 1933, she discovered that he had absconded with the money she had earned in Hollywood—millions of dollars, a fortune at that time. Her bridal attendants were Rudolph Valentino and Pola Negri, one of Valentino's girlfriends whom he referred to on his deathbed that same year as his "bride-to-be." The following year, Pola became Mae's sister-in-law by marrying Count Serge Mdivani.

MAE MURRAY

❧

The Merry Widow, 1925
DIRECTOR AND COSTUME DESIGNER:
ERICH VON STROHEIM

Erich von Stroheim's direction, sets, and costumes made this version of *The Merry Widow* the most opulent as well as the most controversial. Mae Murray always played glamorous blondes, but had limited acting skills. This performance was considered her best because of von Stroheim's strong direction and his emphasis on costuming, which was of major importance to Mae. *The Merry Widow*'s extras included Clark Gable and two of Hollywood's future costume designers: Walter Plunkett (*Gone With the Wind,* 1939) and Irene (*The Postman Always Rings Twice,* 1946).

WEDDING OF PAUL BERN AND JEAN HARLOW, JULY 2, 1932

❦

The competition between studio stars was fierce, especially when it came to their beaus. Norma Shearer had married the second in command at MGM, Irving Thalberg, so Jean Harlow pursued Thalberg's assistant, Paul Bern. Everyone wondered why the "Platinum Blonde" would want to marry MGM's "palace eunuch." On July 2, at 8:30 in the evening, Paul Bern married Harlean Carpenter McGrew in an informal home ceremony. She wore her "lucky" ankle bracelet on her left leg. Ten weeks later Paul Bern committed suicide.

SPENCER TRACY, JEAN HARLOW

❦

Libeled Lady, 1936
DIRECTOR: JACK CONWAY
COSTUME DESIGNER: DOLLY TREE

This is one of the screwiest screwball comedies of the thirties, starring the screen's daffiest sexpot, Jean Harlow. It's another "left at the altar" plot, but Jean doesn't just stay in her gorgeous, slinky gown for laughs; she's brazenly braless and looks incredible! The team of William Powell and Myrna Loy also star, but it was Harlow who was engaged to Powell during the making of *Libeled Lady,* aborting his child when he refused to tie the knot. The following year, Powell and Loy were making the movie *Double Wedding* when the twenty-six-year old Harlow died of uremic poisoning.

LESLIE HOWARD, NORMA SHEARER

Smilin' Through, 1932
DIRECTOR: SIDNEY FRANKLIN
COSTUME DESIGNER: ADRIAN

Smilin' Through, a nominee for Best Picture, was the pivotal film in Shearer's career, making her into a superstar. Norma won the Oscar for best actress in the drama *The Divorcee* (1930), although her husband, Irving Thalberg, thought she couldn't play anything but comedy. He changed his mind when shown the George Hurrell photos of Norma posing seductively, wearing sexy Adrian gowns.

"When Mel [Brooks] told his Jewish mother he was marrying an Italian girl, she said, 'Bring her over. I'll be in the kitchen—with my head in the oven.'" —Anne Bancroft

WEDDING OF NORMA SHEARER AND IRVING THALBERG, SEPTEMBER 29, 1927

The Thalberg wedding took place in the garden of their Sunset Boulevard home, where a flower-covered arbor had been constructed by Cedric Gibbons, the most important production designer in Hollywood's history. Thalberg, the vice president and head of production at MGM, was nicknamed "the Boy Wonder," the title of a short story about him in the *Saturday Evening Post.* During his twelve-year tenure, he personally supervised and produced the wondrous films of MGM's glamour years, but his name rarely appeared on the screen. "Credit you give yourself isn't worth having," said Thalberg.

CLARK GABLE, JOAN CRAWFORD

✣

Forsaking All Others, 1934
DIRECTOR: W. S. VAN DYKE
COSTUME DESIGNER: ADRIAN

Clark never looked so handsome and sexy, Joan was never any more beautiful, and Robert Montgomery was never so wimpy in yet another "gorgeous gal left at the altar" story. MGM's hairstylist, Sydney Guilaroff, said, "One of the hairstyles I created for Joan, which clung to her head, then fanned out in the back, swept the nation as soon as *Forsaking All Others* was shown."

ZASU PITTS, CAROLE LOMBARD

⟡

The Gay Bride, 1934
DIRECTOR: JACK CONWAY
COSTUME DESIGNER: DOLLY TREE

Carole plays a gold-digging showgirl who agrees to marry a rich gangster, but falls for her bodyguard instead. Zasu Pitts, the great silent-film star, plays her older sister. The wedding, the wedding-night negligee, and the going-away suit with orchids from here to there are real "show biz." Like Jean Harlow, Lombard succeeded at being sexy and funny simultaneously. *The Gay Bride* has the same crew as *Libeled Lady*: director Conway, costume designer Tree, and boyfriend-of-the-star William Powell, who was Carole's first husband (1931–1933).

WEDDING OF CAROLE LOMBARD
AND CLARK GABLE,
MARCH 29, 1939

Gable and Lombard got married in Kingman, Arizona, the hometown of Clark's good friend and western sidekick, Andy Devine. The next day, Carole held an open house for the press at her home. Clark waved good-bye and said he'd return in a short while after making a small film, *Gone With the Wind*. In January 1942, Carole flew to her hometown of Fort Wayne, Indiana, for a bond rally; on the return flight, she and her mother were killed when the plane went down near Las Vegas. When Gable died in 1960, his wife, Kay, buried him where he belonged: in Forest Lawn Cemetery in Los Angeles, next to his true love, Carole Lombard.

ORSON WELLES, LORETTA YOUNG

The Stranger, 1946
DIRECTOR: ORSON WELLES
COSTUME DESIGNER: MICHAEL WOULFE

This film was considered to be the least creative of Welles's films, but certainly the most commercial. He plays a Nazi war criminal who is hiding out in Connecticut and about to marry beautiful Loretta Young. Costume designer Michael Woulfe recalled that Mr. Welles asked him to make another costume for Loretta, as the scene with her leaving church early had to be cut and was being replaced with a "walking the dog in the woods" scene. Loretta told Orson that she would never "cut" church, not even in the movies. The churchgoing ensemble she was wearing wouldn't work for a wood walk, but a vicuña coat would.

LORETTA YOUNG, CECIL KELLAWAY

Half Angel, 1951
DIRECTOR: RICHARD SALE
COSTUME DESIGNER: GWEN WAKELING

In this film, Loretta is a prim-and-proper nurse who sleepwalks; and when she does, she flirts outrageously with Joseph Cotten and dresses fashionably, wearing a New Look suit (a longer-length skirt and jacket with padded hips and nipped-in waist). Loretta started acting in movies at the age of four and appeared with all three of her sisters in *The Story of Alexander Graham Bell* (1939). Although she won an Oscar for *The Farmer's Daughter* in 1947, her favorite film was *Ramona* (1936).

ELOPEMENT OF LORETTA YOUNG
AND GRANT WITHERS,
JANUARY 26, 1930

◈

Loretta and good-looking twenties actor Grant Withers appeared together in *The Second Floor Mystery* (1929). He was a womanizer and a heavy drinker, but seventeen-year-old Loretta fell hard. On January 26, the twenty-six-year-old Withers hired a small plane to fly them to Yuma, Arizona, to be married. Loretta's mother, Gladys, was successful in annulling the marriage. Grant committed suicide in 1950.

WEDDING OF LORETTA YOUNG
AND TOM LEWIS,
JULY 31, 1940

෴

Loretta married Tom Lewis, an advertising executive who also had directed her first Screen Guild appearance. On July 31, they married at the Chapel of St. Paul's Church in Westwood. Baby sister Georgiana (now Mrs. Ricardo Montalban) was her maid of honor. Loretta wore lavender tulle, designed by Irene. Afterward, the bridal couple honeymooned in Mexico, where they visited a bullfight and were almost stampeded when Loretta was recognized. Loretta's life-long friend and costume designer, Jean Louis, was her third husband (1993–1997).

JANE WYMAN

Just for You, 1952

DIRECTOR: ELLIOTT NUGENT
COSTUME DESIGNER: EDITH HEAD

In *Just for You*, Bing Crosby is a producer who is much too busy for his children. Jane Wyman, who plays a bride in a Broadway show, urges him to stop and smell the roses. In real life, Jane married four times—including two times to Fred Karger, who worked at Columbia Studios as a voice coach. Marilyn Monroe wanted to marry Fred as well, but he didn't think she'd make a good stepmother.

PUBLICITY PHOTO OF JANE WYMAN

Here Comes the Groom, 1951

DIRECTOR: FRANK CAPRA
COSTUME DESIGNER: EDITH HEAD

Bing Crosby tries to win back his fiancée, Jane Wyman, using two adorable tots as ploys. There's a garden wedding with orchids growing on trees, lots of organdy, and a feisty granny who says, "This is better than television." Louis Armstrong and the great song "In the Cool, Cool, Cool of the Evening" round out a Capra fun fest!

WEDDING OF RONALD REAGAN AND JANE WYMAN, JANUARY 26, 1940

❧

On January 26, a flu-ridden Ronnie Reagan climbed out of his bed, secured a license to marry Jane Wyman, and then went back to bed. The small wedding took place at the Wee Kirk o' the Heather Church in Glendale, California. The bride and groom left immediately for a honeymoon in Palm Springs. "Not many women can say they voted for their ex-husband. Even fewer would want to," said Wyman in later years.

WEDDING OF PIER ANGELI
AND VIC DAMONE,
NOVEMBER 24, 1954

Pier Angeli fell in love with James Dean while he filmed *East of Eden* (1955), but her mother put an end to the relationship because he wasn't Catholic, and then arranged her marriage to crooner Vic Damone. They were married until 1958. Vic married wife number four, Diahann Carroll, in 1987, and then wed fashion designer Rena Rowan in 1998. Pier died of a drug overdose in 1971.

WEDDING OF AUDREY HEPBURN AND MEL FERRER, SEPTEMBER 25, 1954

❧

Audrey and Mel got married in Burgenstock, Switzerland. She wore an ankle-length Givenchy gown of white organdy with puff sleeves and a billowy skirt. And sitting atop her pixie do was a crown of white roses. The couple divorced in 1968. The following year, when Audrey married Andrea Dotti, Givenchy designed a long-sleeved mini dress in pink jersey, with matching tights, for her to wear. "Think pink!"

FRED ASTAIRE, AUDREY HEPBURN

❧

Funny Face, 1957
DIRECTOR: STANLEY DONEN
COSTUME DESIGNERS: EDITH HEAD
AND GIVENCHY (FOR AUDREY HEPBURN)

Funny Face is Hollywood's greatest homage to the fashion world, with Astaire playing a Richard Avedon–type photographer, Kay Thompson playing a Diana Vreeland–type fashion magazine editor, models Suzy Parker and Dovima playing Suzy Parker and Dovima, and adorable Audrey playing adorable Audrey. Edith Head created the "beatnik look" for the New York Audrey; then, when she gets to Paris, her good friend and confidant Hubert de Givenchy designed her costumes. The wedding scene was so ephemerally blissful that no one seemed to mind the age difference between Fred and Audrey.

JANE RUSSELL, MARILYN MONROE

❧

Gentlemen Prefer Blondes, 1953

DIRECTOR: HOWARD HAWKS
COSTUME DESIGNER: TRAVILLA

Marilyn Monroe, as showgirl Lorelei Lee, and Jane Russell, as her wisecracking friend Dorothy, are looking for love, money, and gorgeous clothes. So they go on a Paris shopping spree to Schiaparelli, Dior, and Balenciaga. Their double wedding is a shipboard affair with identical Travilla-designed, ballerina-length dresses. Bill Travilla was responsible for most of Marilyn's memorable costumes, including the famous *Seven Year Itch* (1955) dress, which he selected "off the rack" in a small store in New York, near that famous subway grate.

WEDDING OF NORMA JEAN BAKER (MARILYN MONROE) AND JAMES DOUGHERTY, JUNE 19, 1942

❧

Just a few weeks after Marilyn's sixteenth birthday, she married James Dougherty in Westwood at the home of one of her husband's buddies. Jim was movie-star handsome and had been a classmate of Jane Russell's. The house had a winding staircase, as the bride wanted, even at that age, to make a grand entrance. Her gown, made of eyelet lace, was handsewn by her aunt. Marilyn's mom was unable to attend, as she was committed to a sanitarium in San Francisco. The marriage lasted three years. In 2001, Marilyn's half sister, Berniece Miracle, offered Marilyn's wedding gown at Sotheby's auction house. Its sleeves had been removed when it was worn by Mona Miracle (Berniece's daughter) on her first date.

WEDDING OF JOE DIMAGGIO AND MARILYN MONROE, JANUARY 14, 1954

Marilyn started dating Yankee slugger Joe DiMaggio during the filming of *Gentlemen Prefer Blondes*. One morning, Joe whisked her off to City Hall, saying, "Let's get married." When he realized that it was Friday the thirteenth, he postponed the marriage until the next day. Marilyn wore a dark-brown suit with an ermine collar that was designed by a friend, New York designer Ceil Chapman. Joe gave her a mink coat as a wedding gift. The marriage lasted only eight months; but after Marilyn's death in 1962 of a supposed sedative overdose, Joe put fresh roses at her memorial site for years. Hugh Hefner, who bought the rights to Marilyn's nude calendar and made it the feature attraction of *Playboy*'s first issue (December 1953), owns the burial vault next to hers.

WEDDING OF MARILYN MONROE AND ARTHUR MILLER, JUNE 29, 1956

Marilyn met playwright Arthur Miller while she was in New York, working with her drama coach, Lee Strasberg. Before the wedding, Marilyn stayed with Arthur and his parents in his seventeenth-century farmhouse in Roxbury, Connecticut. It was there that she not only took conversion courses from a rabbi, but also learned about a major Jewish pastime from Arthur's mom: cooking traditional dishes such as chicken soup with matzo balls and chopped liver. When asked about Marilyn's Judaic instructions, Arthur's sister said, "I took piano lessons. That doesn't make me a concert pianist." Of course, Marilyn was late for the wedding, arriving in jeans and then changing to a beige dress with a beige veil, which she had personally dipped in coffee to match. The couple divorced in 1961.

LEE BOWMAN AND RITA HAYWORTH

Cover Girl, 1944

DIRECTOR: CHARLES VIDOR
COSTUME DESIGNERS: TRAVIS BANTON,
MURIEL KING, AND GWEN WAKELING

Rita Hayworth plays the dual roles of Rusty, who follows her quest to become a cover girl, and her own grandmother, seen in in flashbacks. There is the Kern-Gershwin score, Gene Kelly, great clothes, even greater hats, sequins, furs, jewels, and Eve Arden, the forever wisecracking fashion editor. Who knew that America was in the midst of World War II? An unhappy Rita marries Lee Bowman while wearing pale lavender chiffon and carrying pink roses and gladioli. The bridesmaids and Eve, as the maid of honor, are a Technicolor fantasy in green and fuschia.

WEDDING OF ORSON WELLES AND RITA HAYWORTH (JOSEPH COTTEN, BEST MAN), SEPTEMBER 7, 1943

In the middle of shooting *Cover Girl,* Rita eloped with Orson Welles. The press called the match "the beauty and the brain"—like they had that of Marilyn Monroe and Arthur Miller. At lunchtime, Rita and Orson drove to Santa Monica to pick up *Citizen Kane*'s Joseph Cotten, who was their best man. During the ceremony, Welles had trouble removing the ring from the box, and was so nervous that he couldn't get it on Rita's ring finger. Rita cried with joy, or with pain, and kissed Orson several times. According to costar Lee Bowman, Rita arrived back on the set looking very sheepish, but didn't "tell." The film's wedding scene was, coincidentally, shot that day. Rita and Orson divorced in 1948.

WEDDING OF ALY KHAN AND RITA HAYWORTH,
MAY 27, 1949

༆

Rita Hayworth and Aly Khan's wedding reception was held at the prince's home, Château l'Horizon, where 200 gallons of cologne filled the pool and flowers spelled out Margarita (Rita's real name) and Aly. A few days later, copies of Rita's Jacques Fath wedding dress were for sale in department stores across the United States. The copy, by Roseweb Frocks, was available in black, brown, or "bride's blue" for a mere $18.74. Rita and Aly divorced in 1953. Their daughter, Princess Yasmin, has become a viable force in the fight against Alzheimer's, the disease that claimed her mom's life in 1987.

BETTY HUTTON, EDDIE BRACKEN

The Miracle of Morgan's Creek, 1944
DIRECTOR: PRESTON STURGES
COSTUME DESIGNER: EDITH HEAD

Diana Lynn, who plays Betty's younger sis, spends her time playing "The Wedding March" on the piano. She says, "It doesn't cost anything to think about marriage and it only costs two dollars to do it." Eddie Bracken wears a vintage World War I military uniform for the wedding, and buys Betty a gardenia corsage for ten cents. Although her wedding attire is conservative, this Sturges comedy is wonderful and wacky, and so is twenty-three-year-old Betty Hutton. Who else but Trudy Kockenlocker (Betty) could have quintuplets and not know how it happened?

WEDDING OF BETTY HUTTON AND TED BRISKIN, SEPTEMBER 3, 1945

Betty and wealthy Chicago businessman Ted Briskin enjoyed themselves at the wedding reception Betty's mom gave for them at the Beverly Hills Hotel. Betty quickly rebounded from her relationship with married director Sidney Lanfield, who she now claims was the "love of her life." Although Briskin opened a branch of his business in Los Angeles, the marriage ended in 1950.

MARY PICKFORD, DOUGLAS FAIRBANKS

The Taming of the Shrew, 1929
DIRECTOR: SAM TAYLOR
COSTUME DESIGNER: MITCHELL LEISEN

The fourth screen adaptation of *The Taming of the Shrew* starred America's first sweetheart, Mary Pickford, and her husband, Douglas Fairbanks. This film, their only one together, had the infamous credit "By William Shakespeare with additional dialogue by Sam Taylor." Mary and Doug, along with Charlie Chaplin, formed one of the earliest film studios, United Artists. They were married in New York, where Mary met Travis Banton, who made her wedding gown. Banton went to Hollywood at Mary's request, and first worked with studio head Adolphe Zukor, designing furs for his early films. Before the movies, Zukor had been a furrier and wanted to keep the fur industry alive, just in case the movies failed. Mary and Doug were married from 1920 until 1936. In 1937, she married Buddy Rogers.

RICHARD BURTON, ELIZABETH TAYLOR

The Taming of the Shrew, 1967
DIRECTOR: FRANCO ZEFFIRELLI
COSTUME DESIGNERS: IRENE SHARAFF
AND DANILO DONATI

Costume designer Irene Sharaff said that Liz Taylor's Shakespeare was so natural that the verse sounded like real conversation. The wedding is the high point of the film: it's a slugfest that ends with the drunken Burton falling sound asleep. Richard was married to Liz twice. In 1968, Burton wrote in his diary: "I have been inordinately lucky all my life; but the greatest luck of all has been Elizabeth. She is a wildly exciting lover-mistress, she is shy and witty, she is nobody's fool, she is a brilliant actress, beautiful beyond the dreams of pornography . . . AND SHE LOVES ME."

NATALIE WOOD

❧

Penelope, 1966
DIRECTOR: ARTHUR HILLER
COSTUME DESIGNER: EDITH HEAD

Penelope (Natalie Wood), looking for attention, robs her husband's bank wearing a Givenchy suit. When she confesses to her shrink, Dick Shawn, he tells her to get rid of the suit. Natalie says, "You can't just throw a Givenchy down a manhole." The comedians, including Jonathan Winters, are very funny and the fashion is *ultra* fashionable, especially in the wedding scene: Edith Head's budget was a quarter of a million dollars!

NATALIE WOOD, C. 1958

❦

PUBLICITY PHOTO

When Natalie was five, she appeared in a bit part in *Happy Land* (1943), making a big impression on the director when she burst out crying because she dropped her ice-cream cone. She easily made the transition from child star to young adult, and, although the *Harvard Lampoon* initiated its annual "Natalie Wood Award" for the worst performance–she was nominated for an Oscar three times, including *Rebel Without a Cause* (1955).

WEDDING OF NATALIE WOOD AND ROBERT WAGNER, DECEMBER 28, 1957

❦

Robert Wagner, originally from a prominent Detroit family, asked Natalie Wood's father for her hand in marriage before proposing. Then R.J. and Natalie went to the Mocambo for dinner, where, inside her glass of champagne, there was an engagement ring. Three weeks later, a dozen people watched them get married in a church in Scottsdale, Arizona. Nineteen-year-old Natalie wore a gown of white lace and seed pearls with a lace mantilla. The couple divorced in 1962. Each of them remarried other people, but then, in 1972, R.J. and Natalie married for the second time, aboard a chartered yacht. Natalie said, "R.J. and I are settling down for good. The first marriage was just a rehearsal for the second one. Neither of us will ever marry again." Natalie drowned in 1981, and R.J. married family friend Jill St. John in 1991.

JULIA ROBERTS

Steel Magnolias, 1989
DIRECTOR: HERBERT ROSS
COSTUME DESIGNER: JULIE WEISS

Based on a Broadway play, this film is the story of six women who participate in full-time Southern belle coffee-klatching. How can you resist a movie with lines like "Time marches on and sooner or later you realize it is marching across your face" (Dolly Parton) and "The church looks like it's been hosed down with Pepto-Bismol" (Sally Field), together with a wedding cake shaped like an armadillo? Oscar nominee Julia Roberts wore a wedding gown that according to designer Julie Weiss "was born from a Civil War dress . . . a tightly fitted bodice, a hoop, a bustle, a crinoline, and, of course, a bow."

JULIA ROBERTS

Runaway Bride, 1999
DIRECTOR: GARRY MARSHALL
COSTUME DESIGNER: ALBERT WOLSKY

This time, Julia Roberts plays a hardware-store owner in a small town who leaves lots of guys at the altar. Costume designer Albert Wolsky made all of Julia's wedding gowns for the five weddings, as well as many copies of each, as Julia had to perform different getaways and look perfect at the same time. For example, when she wears the most classic of the gowns, Albert had to use a stretch fabric, allowing her to climb out of a window. In another scene, she runs out of the church with a small boy on her train, which had to be longer and stronger to pull him without ripping.

WEDDING OF JULIA ROBERTS AND LYLE LOVETT,
JUNE 27, 1993

Julia Roberts, who was born in Smyrna, Georgia, and country music singer/songwriter Lyle Lovett surprised everyone with their quickie marriage: they had been dating for only three weeks. Lyle selected Julia's designer dress, by Comme des Garçons, but, obviously, forgot to buy her shoes. The wedding was in Marion, Indiana, where Lyle was performing. Their marriage ended in 1995.

THE *More* THE *Merrier*

BEFORE THE DAYS OF *People* AND *In Style*, THERE WERE FAN MAGAZINES SUCH AS *Modern Screen* AND *Photoplay*, AND TWO GOSSIP COLUMNISTS WHO WERE ARCHRIVALS: LOUELLA PARSONS AND HEDDA HOPPER. HEDDA DESCRIBED THE DIFFERENCE BETWEEN THEM: "LOUELLA PARSONS IS A REPORTER TRYING TO BE A HAM; HEDDA HOPPER IS A HAM TRYING TO BE A REPORTER." LOUELLA, WHO WAS FAMOUS FOR HER "SCOOPS" FOR THE HEARST NEWSPAPERS, WROTE THE FOLLOWING ARTICLE ABOUT THE "WEDDING OF THE YEAR" IN JUNE OF 1937 FOR THE *Los Angeles Examiner*:

JEANETTE AND GENE MARRIED

As reverently beautiful as a picture from a medieval princess storybook was the scene at Wilshire Methodist Episcopal Church last night as titian-haired Jeanette MacDonald became the bride of Gene Raymond.

Inside the church were gathered all the friends of Jeanette and Gene—those who loved them and who have watched this romance since it started over a year ago. Outside were more than 10,000 loyal well-wishers and fans, who gathered to call friendly greetings to the stars who were invited, and to cheer the bridal party.

Jeanette was radiant in her Adrian designed bridal gown of flesh pink mousseline over delicate pink taffeta. . . . The long veil over the bride's beautiful flaming hair was pink tulle. The cap was edged with flowers, . . . and the bridal train was probably the longest ever seen in Hollywood, even in a picture. . . . The inspirational voice of Nelson Eddy, Jeanette's co-star in many of her finest films, rang out with the heart-stirring "I Love You Truly."

A gasp of admiration went up as the colorful bridal party, including Fay Wray and Ginger Rogers, came up the aisle, looking like flowers in their pink frost crepe gowns, fashioned in Grecian style. Each wore small pink frost caps surrounded by baby's breath, and they wore mousseline sheer coats over their gowns.

Among the guests and what they wore were:

- Mrs. Harold Lloyd, white crepe gown with matching jacket, white orchid corsage, pearls.

- Mrs. Harry Martin (Louella Parsons), white gown of Chantilly lace, with small white turban. Ermine cape and pearls.

- Irene Hervey, blue chiffon Chanel model with very full pleated skirt. Long chiffon cape of Wallis blue lined with silver. White orchids and diamonds.

- Mrs. Hal Roach, Hattie Carnegie gown of white net fashioned with full skirt, low square neck and short pouf sleeves. Short sable coat, white orchids and pearls.

- Loretta Young, white satin gown with hoop skirt. Worn with white fox bolero and pearls.

- Joan Bennett, pale gray chiffon gown with billowy skirt and shirred bodice. Soft crushed girdle of chartreuse taffeta and worn with diamond clips and bracelets and a knee length cape of silver fox.

- Ann Sothern, silver tissue cloth frock with molded bodice and full flowing skirt. Rubies and a silver fox jacket.

- Mrs. George Hurrell, pale pink taffeta with a fitted bodice and a full skirt embroidered with beauvais roses. Diamonds and a white fox cape.

Today, the public doesn't need long, written descriptions about celebrity weddings. These events, with their multitudes of guests, gifts, flowers, and designer duds, are brought into our homes via television. And because of the enormous emphasis on Oscar dressing and the public's recognition of designer names, just one or two little words by the media, such as Versace or Calvin Klein, says it all.

Previous page

WEDDING OF GENE RAYMOND AND JEANETTE MACDONALD, JUNE 16, 1937

ZASU PITTS, CHESTER CONKLIN

Greed, 1925

DIRECTOR: ERICH VON STROHEIM

The film's wedding takes place in the rooms Zasu and Chester have rented, which are very cramped, but filled with flowers. Outside, a funeral procession passes by and mourning music can be heard along with the chirping of two lovebirds, a wedding gift. For two hours, the bridal party and their guests gorge themselves; it's just your typical wedding feast! Von Stroheim's film was originally nine hours, longer than some Hollywood marriages.

LESLIE HOWARD, VIVIEN LEIGH, OLIVIA DE HAVILLAND

Gone With the Wind, 1939

DIRECTORS: VICTOR FLEMING, GEORGE CUKOR, SAM WOOD
COSTUME DESIGNER: WALTER PLUNKETT

In Margaret Mitchell's novel, Scarlett wore her mother's dress, and because she married so quickly, there was no time for alterations. Because designer Plunkett specialized in historical costuming, he translated the book's descriptions to a tee. Vivien Leigh's dress was supposed to look dated, costly, and too long for her, as her mother had married twenty-five years earlier, was taller, and came from a very wealthy family. The gown is gorgeous, but the scene is much too short to admire it. Scarlett's husband dies shortly after the wedding, but she refuses to wear her widow's weeds—dark clothes and veil for mourning—and instead insists on wearing a fuscia feathered hat! After all, tomorrow is another day.

ORSON WELLES, RUTH WARRICK, AND GUESTS

Citizen Kane, 1941

DIRECTOR: ORSON WELLES
COSTUME DESIGNER: EDWARD STEVENSON

Twenty-five-year-old director Orson Welles supposedly modeled his character Charles Foster Kane on William Randolph Hearst: his life, his love, and Xanadu, his home. When Kane (Welles) married Emily Norton (Ruth Warrick) in 1916, it was announced that she was the president's niece. "Before he's through, she'll be the president's wife," was the buzz. That didn't happen; Emily died with their son two years later. Their wedding was shown in a newsreel clip after Kane's death. Ruth has played Phoebe Tyler on *All My Children* since 1970.

WEDDING OF JOHN WAYNE AND JOSEPHINE SAENZ (LORETTA YOUNG, MAID OF HONOR), JUNE 1933

Former football player John Wayne and Josephine Saenz, daughter of the Panamanian consul, were married at the home of Loretta Young in Bel Air. John had four children with Josephine and three children by his third wife, Pilar Palette. In 1979, the year he died, he made a guest appearance on TV's *Rowan & Martin's Laugh-in* wearing a fluffy pink bunny suit.

JOHN WAYNE, MAUREEN O'HARA

The Quiet Man, 1952
DIRECTOR: JOHN FORD
COSTUME DESIGNER: ADELE PALMER

The Quiet Man was the first major film shot in Ireland. John Wayne plays an American who goes to Ireland to reclaim his past. He meets and marries Maureen O'Hara, who looks beautiful in a white-and-lavender wedding gown. Barry Fitzgerald has the movie's best line: the morning after, when seeing the broken bridal bed, he says, "Impetuous!" The film was a family affair. Maureen brought her new baby and the baby's nurse to Ireland, and all four of John Wayne's children made an appearance in the movie.

JAMES STEWART, CARY GRANT, KATHARINE HEPBURN

❧

The Philadelphia Story, 1940
DIRECTOR: GEORGE CUKOR
COSTUME DESIGNER: ADRIAN

The All-American comedy classic: who loves who, who get's who, and who wore what??? Tracy Lord, played by Katharine Hepburn, wears jodhpurs, belted pantsuits, and, at one point, a striped bathing suit with a floor-length Grecian cover-up. Hepburn's even fashionable when wet! Kate wanted Clark Gable and Spencer Tracy as her costars even though she hadn't met either of them at the time. Gable refused and was replaced by Cary Grant, who got top billing and a fee of $137,000, which was paid to the British War Relief. Oh yes, the wedding: Kate, Cary, and Jimmy are shocked by the flash of a camera from a mystery guest.

WEDDING OF GLORIA AND JIMMY STEWART, AUGUST 9, 1949

❧

Hollywood's beloved bachelor, 41-year-old Jimmy Stewart, married Washington socialite Gloria McLean, a divorcée with two sons who was ten years his junior. Prior to Pearl Harbor, the popular actor enlisted in the service, the first movie star to do so (he barely made the cut as he was five pounds underweight). He received the Distinguished Flying Cross, among other honors, eventually becoming a Air Force colonel and, in 1959, a brigadier general. The Stewarts' wedding was at a church in Brentwood, California, where Jimmy's dad was on the fund-raising committee and, after the ceremony, approached all the guests for contributions. Their twin daughters were born two years later. Jimmy met Gloria when he was seated next to her at a dinner party given by the Gary Coopers. After her death in 1994 he rarely left his home.

HERBERT MARSHALL, ANNE BAXTER, JOHN PAYNE,
GENE TIERNEY, CLIFTON WEBB

❧

The Razor's Edge, 1946
DIRECTOR: EDMUND GOULDING
COSTUME DESIGNER: OLEG CASSINI

Gene Tierney's true love in this film is Tyrone Power, who leaves for Europe to "find himself" and the meaning of life. Gene, on the rebound, marries John Payne. Her friend, played by Anne Baxter, goes through hard times and is found and saved in Paris by Tyrone, who offers to marry her and buy her a wedding gown at the couture salon of Molyneux. Marry that man! Anne, architect Frank Lloyd Wright's granddaughter, won the Oscar for Best Supporting Actress.

BETTY GRABLE, CESAR ROMERO

That Lady in Ermine, 1948

DIRECTOR: ERNST LUBITSCH
COSTUME DESIGNER: RENÉ HUBERT

Betty Grable plays a double role in this film: one is Angelina, the great-great-great-granddaughter of the sixteenth-century Lady in Ermine, a fictional character, and the other is the Lady in Ermine herself. The sixteenth-century Betty marries Cesar Romero just as the enemy arrives. She also lifts all her hoops and petticoats, allowing her twentieth-century fans to see those famous legs. In real life, Betty was married to bandleader Harry James from 1943 until 1965. She was buried in 1973, on what would have been their thirtieth wedding anniversary, and Harry died ten years later, on what would have been their fortieth.

WEDDING OF HARRY JAMES AND BETTY GRABLE, JULY 5, 1943

Betty Grable and her bridesmaid, Betty Furness, who later became TV's Westinghouse spokesperson, traveled on a non-air-conditioned train from Los Angeles to Las Vegas. The trip took twelve hours, and Grable, wearing a yellow suit, arrived in such a wilted state that a new wedding dress had to be purchased. She wore an ice blue dress and carried a lace hanky, a gift from Alice Faye. Although their marriage was at four in the morning, it attracted throngs of fans. After the ceremony, Betty called her mom, whose first question was "How many photographers were there?" One photographer shooting the newly married couple was Frank Powolney, who also took Betty's famous pinup picture.

ROBERT RYAN, CLAUDETTE COLBERT

The Secret Fury, 1950
DIRECTOR: MEL FERRER
COSTUME DESIGNER: HATTIE CARNEGIE FOR CLAUDETTE COLBERT

Robert and Claudette's wedding is interrupted by a man in the back row, who says that he knows a reason why these two should not be joined in holy wedlock—that Colbert is married to someone else. Her fabulous wedding gown is from Hattie Carnegie, the New York–based design house that mostly copied French couture creations for their American clientele.

FRANK SINATRA, VIVIAN BLAINE, JEAN SIMMONS, MARLON BRANDO

❧

Guys and Dolls, 1955

DIRECTOR: JOSEPH L. MANKIEWICZ
COSTUME DESIGNER: IRENE SHARAFF

Guys and Dolls was slick Hollywood doing Broadway, only much bigger. The entire town was invited to the wedding, and the "Hot Box" girls are the bridesmaids, wearing pink and orange satin; the gangster groomsmen are wearing zoot suits. Brando had three wives, all "island girls." *Photoplay* magazine reported that when Marlon and Anna Kashfi took their vows, a couple by the name of O'Callaghan came forward to say that their daughter, Anna, was Irish and not Indian. Had Marlon known, he may have lost interest.

"When I say, 'I do,' the justice of the peace replies, 'I know, I know.' I'm the only man in the world whose marriage license reads 'To Whom It May Concern.'" —Mickey Rooney

WEDDING OF AVA GARDNER AND ARTIE SHAW, OCTOBER 17, 1945

Ava told Lana Turner, "Of course I married Artie Shaw; everybody married Artie Shaw." He was Lana's first husband and Ava's second. Her first was Mickey Rooney (1941–1943), and her third was Frank Sinatra (1951–1957). Ava and Shaw were divorced the next year. Much later she reminisced, "All I ever got out of any of my marriages was the two years Artie Shaw financed on an analyst's couch."

AVA GARDNER, ROSSANO BRAZZI, HUMPHREY BOGART

❧

The Barefoot Contessa, 1954
DIRECTOR: JOSEPH L. MANKIEWICZ
COSTUME DESIGNER: FONTANA

When Spanish dancer/Hollywood star Maria (Ava) marries into Italian royalty, the ceremony takes place in an ancient chapel followed by two very different receptions. Ava yearns to be at the town's celebration of the marriage, complete with dancing and drinking. Instead, she is forced to attend a formal reception with her new husband, Count Vincenzo (Brazzi), and his stodgy family. Only her good friend, played by Bogey, was there to comfort her. . . . Nevertheless, she looked sensational in a gown designed by the leading couturieres of Italy in the fifties: the Fontana sisters.

BING CROSBY, GRACE KELLY, SIDNEY BLACKMER

High Society, 1956

DIRECTOR: CHARLES WALTERS
COSTUME DESIGNER: HELEN ROSE

This is the Cole Porter musical version of *The Philadelphia Story*, with great stars, great songs, and designer Helen Rose's homage to the original Adrian costumes: jodhpurs and a rolled-sleeve shirt, and a white pleated beach cover over a halter neck swim dress. The pièce de résistance? *The wedding dress:* blush organdy with embroidered flowers. But the bride and groom don't seem terribly happy, although this is their second go-around. Could it be that it's past Bing's bedtime . . . and that newly betrothed Grace is worried about how to decorate the palace in Monaco?

WEDDING OF PRINCE RAINIER AND GRACE KELLY, APRIL 19, 1956

In 1956, Grace's gown, designed by Helen Rose, was given to the Philadelphia Museum of Art, along with two of the bridesmaid dresses designed by Priscilla of Boston and a flower girl dress from Neiman Marcus. In order to display Grace's gown, the Philadelphia Museum has to use their smallest mannequin because Grace had a twenty-one-inch waist at the time of her wedding. She wore her real engagement ring, a 12-carat emerald-cut diamond, during the filming of *High Society*.

WEDDING AND HONEYMOON OF KATHY GRANT AND BING CROSBY, OCTOBER 1957

In July 1955, reporters discovered that Kathryn Grant had ordered a wedding gown and, after reading about it in the newspapers, Bing blew. However, wedding banns were posted at the Church of the Good Shepherd, where Kathy was taking instructions in the Catholic faith. Her conversion didn't take place until two years later, and was followed shortly by the wedding.

TYRONE POWER, KIM NOVAK

❧

The Eddy Duchin Story, 1956
DIRECTOR: GEORGE SIDNEY
COSTUME DESIGNER: JEAN LOUIS

For this film, Tyrone Power learned how to play the piano, Eddy Duchin style, in just three months. He actually played some of the numbers (others are dubbed by Carmen Cavallero). Kim Novak looks like a dream with her short curly hair and classic Jean Louis gowns, similar to those Jean designed for Loretta Young as she twirled into our homes via her TV show from 1953 to 1961. For the wedding, Kim wears white satin and the bridesmaids are in ice blue with cerise hats and flowers. The wedding cake is ice blue decorated with music notes.

WEDDING OF LINDA CHRISTIAN AND TYRONE POWER, JANUARY 27, 1949

Twenty-five-year-old Linda Christian was born in Mexico and married Tyrone Power in a regal ceremony in Rome, wearing a gown designed by the Fontana sisters. Linda began her career as a "Goldwyn Girl" and made twenty-seven movies. The marriage lasted six years.

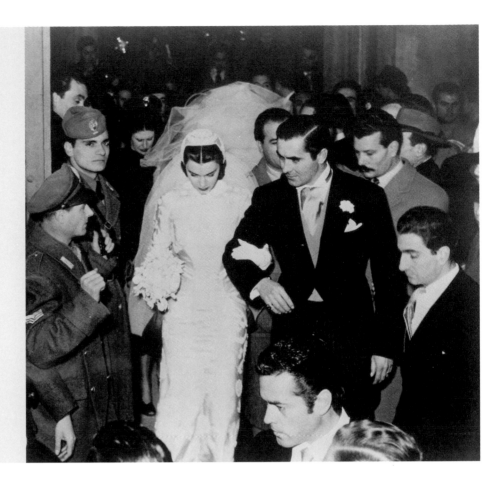

JAMES MASON, LYNN REDGRAVE

Georgy Girl, 1966

DIRECTOR: SILVIO NARIZZANO
COSTUME DESIGNER: MARY QUANT
FOR CHARLOTTE RAMPLING

The Oscar-nominated song "Georgy Girl" provides the London mood of the sixties when we meet plainly plump Lynn Redgrave, her fashionista roommate, the svelte Charlotte Rampling (costumed by the original "mod" designer, Mary Quant), and James Mason, the aging married man who is in lust with Lynn.

ALBERT BROOKS, GOLDIE HAWN

❧

Private Benjamin, 1980
DIRECTOR: HOWARD ZIEFF
COSTUME DESIGNER: BETSY COX

As the film begins, Goldie, in her Oscar-nominated role as Judy Benjamin, is getting married and wearing a typical eighties gown that according to costume designer Betsy Cox, looked "just like a cake topper." In the midst of her conservative Jewish wedding to conservative Albert Brooks, the groom takes Goldie outside, pushes her into a parked car, and asks her to "relieve his stress." They later repeat the act in their hotel room, causing him to expire. Goldie goes from bride to widow in the first ten minutes of this hysterically funny film.

ARMAND ASSANTE, GOLDIE HAWN

❧

Private Benjamin, 1980
DIRECTOR: HOWARD ZIEFF
COSTUME DESIGNER: BETSY COX

Goldie has joined the army, then transfers to NATO in Paris, where she falls for Assante and allows him to change her image: her hair becomes red, and her wedding gown is the height of French fashion, although it was purchased at Bendels in New York City by the costume designer.

BILLY CRYSTAL, BRUNO KIRBY, CARRIE FISHER, MEG RYAN

❧

When Harry Met Sally, 1989
DIRECTOR: ROB REINER
COSTUME DESIGNER: GLORIA GRESHAM

The bride here is Carrie Fisher, daughter of Debbie Reynolds and Eddie Fisher, the lovebirds of the fifties. Costume designer Gloria Gresham said that Fisher kept the wedding gown, claiming that it was nicer than the one she wore when she married Paul Simon in 1983. The "real" couples in the movie telling why they are in love are not real at all. The "real" ones couldn't act "real."

SIOBHAN FALLON, SALMA HAYEK, MATTHEW PERRY, JON TENNEY

❧

Fools Rush In, 1997
DIRECTOR: ANDY TENNANT
COSTUME DESIGNER:
KIMBERLY A. TILLMAN

A one-night stand in Vegas results in a pregnancy and a marriage between perfect strangers: Hayek, who is the first major Mexican star since Dolores del Rio; and Perry, the star of TV's *Friends.* Their first wedding is in a twenty-four-hour chapel, with an Elvis look-alike escorting Hayek down the aisle. She's wearing a T-shirt, a denim miniskirt, and a veil. The second wedding is on an Indian reservation in the Grand Canyon with both families in attendance. Salma made designer Kim Tillman an honorary Mexican because she loved the Frida Kahlo look Tillman gave her. Salma plays the Mexican artist in *Frida* (2002).

IF I KNEW
You Were Coming

In *Runaway Bride* (1999), Julia Roberts's father says, "Wedding cake freezes, this we know." Yes, we do know. In 1998, a memorabilia collector paid $26,000 at an auction for one piece of the Duke and Duchess of Windsor's wedding cake from 1937.

The wedding cake and the cake-cutting ceremony started in ancient Rome, where the ritual of throwing cake crumbs over the bride was said to ensure fertility. Guests would gather around, trying to catch some crumbs and share the bride's good fortune.

The enormous and expensive cakes of today stemmed from the royal weddings of the past. In 1840, Queen Victoria's cake weighed three hundred pounds and was topped with an ice sculpture of Britannia. In 1947, Queen Elizabeth's cake was nine feet tall and weighed five hundred pounds. In 1981, her son, Charles, and his beautiful bride, Diana, had a five-tiered cake that was a new shape for the twentieth century—hexagonal. In 1956, Prince Rainier of Monaco cut his wedding cake with a six-foot sword, as Princess Grace and six hundred star-studded guests watched.

Sylvia Weinstock, the celebrity cake diva, said that although she has baked and decorated most all of the celebrity cakes, "everyone who walks in my door is a star." Sylvia said that her female clients tell their betrothed that the cakes costs less, and then tell their friends that it costs more. Although she signs letters of confidentiality regarding the wedding details, she proudly lists some of her star clients:

Alec Baldwin and Kim Basinger, Michael Douglas and Catherine Zeta-Jones, Liam Neeson and Natasha Richardson, and The Trumps: "The Donald" and Ivana and "The Donald" and Marla Maples, cakes for both marriages.

Sylvia started creating her wedding cakes in the mid seventies, when wedding cakes were mostly frosted in white with a bride-and-groom cake topper. Her creativity doesn't stop with the outside decoration. She reminds her bridal couples, "Don't forget, cake is to be eaten." For Eddie and Nicole Murphy's wedding, she baked a different flavor for each tier: one layer was yellow cake with strawberries, whipped cream, and banana filling; the next was chocolate cake with mocha mousse filling, followed by carrot cake with a cream cheese filling and a yellow cake with lemon mousse and raspberries. The five-foot-high cake was completely covered in sugar flowers with two brown sugar hummingbirds as the cake topper.

One of Hollywood's more unusual cakes is the wedding cake in *Addams Family Values* (1993). When the dancer in the cake doesn't pop out, Gomez asks Lurch, "Was she in the cake before you baked it?"

Previous page

WEDDING OF PRISCILLA BEAULIEU AND ELVIS PRESLEY, MAY 1, 1967

🐦

Elvis Presley, thirty-two years of age and the highest-salaried entertainer in the world, married twenty-one-year-old Priscilla Anne Beaulieu at the Aladdin Hotel in Las Vegas at 9:00 A.M. The bride and groom had an eight-year romance, two years longer than their marriage. Elvis wore a black brocade tux and western boots, while Priscilla wore a gown of her own design that Elvis approved because it completely covered all of her. Baby Lisa Marie arrived nine months later.

FRANK LAWTON,
MAUREEN O'SULLIVAN

❧

David Copperfield, 1935

DIRECTOR: GEORGE CUKOR
COSTUME DESIGNER: DOLLY TREE

This is the beautiful screen adaptation of Charles Dickens's novel, starring Frank Lawton and Maureen O'Sullivan as the adult David and Dora, shown here at their much-too-short wedding reception. Maureen starred opposite Olympic swimmer Johnny Weissmuller in *Tarzan, the Ape Man* (1932). Five other Tarzan films followed; in each one, Jane's body became more covered, as the Legion of Decency was then passing judgment on the amount of bare skin allowed on the silver screen. Maureen married director John Farrow and had seven children, including daughter Mia.

WEDDING OF JOAN BLONDELL
AND DICK POWELL, 1936

Dick and Joan costarred in Warner's backstage musicals for ten years, longer than their nine-year marriage. One of Joan's early roles was Schatzi in *The Greeks Had a Word for Them* (1932), which was the same role that Lauren Bacall played in the remake *How to Marry a Millionaire* (1953). One year after the release of their film *I Want a Divorce* (1940), Dick and Joan separated. Following her divorce from Powell, Joan married Mike Todd, who is best known for his marriage to Liz Taylor. Dick was married to June Allyson from 1945 until his death in 1963.

RUBY KEELER, DICK POWELL

Flirtation Walk, 1934

DIRECTOR: FRANK BORZAGE
COSTUME DESIGNER: ORRY-KELLY

In *Flirtation Walk,* Dick Powell sings "Mr. and Mrs. Is the Name." His costar, Ruby Keeler, married Al Jolson in 1928, but her most popular "marriage" was to her film partner Dick Powell, who appeared with her in many Warner musicals. In *The Wedding Planner* (2001), Jennifer Lopez watches this film's wedding scene while pining over Matthew McConaughey.

MATTHEW MCCONAUGHEY, JENNIFER LOPEZ

The Wedding Planner, 2001

DIRECTOR: ADAM SHANKMAN
COSTUME DESIGNER: PAMELA WITHERS

Jennifer Lopez breaks the First Commandment of Wedding Planners: "Thou shalt not get involved with the groom." She does . . . and he does . . . and they (the bride and groom) don't! But in September 2001, the pop diva married choreographer Cris Judd, wearing a chantilly lace Valentino wedding gown. Donatella Versace gave the couple a honeymoon and a wedding dinner at her villa on Lake Como in Italy. The cake was so big it wouldn't fit through the front door!

GLENN FORD, BETTE DAVIS

❧

A Stolen Life, 1946

DIRECTOR: CURTIS BERNHARDT
COSTUME DESIGNER: ORRY-KELLY

Bette Davis times two means double trouble! She plays twins who are rivals in love. One of them marries Glenn Ford—but which one? Costume designer Orry-Kelly came from Australia and befriended Cary Grant, who promised to get him into the movies, but he wound up behind the screen, creating some of Hollywood's most beloved costumes, including those in *Casablanca* (1942) and *Some Like It Hot* (1959).

WEDDING OF WILLIAM GRANT SHERRY AND BETTE DAVIS, NOVEMBER 29, 1945

❧

In the movie *A Stolen Life* (1946), one of the twins, played by Bette Davis, has a relationship with a rough-and-tough artist, Dane Clark. It was during that time that Bette started dating William Grant Sherry, a former boxer turned painter, whom she had met when he was on leave from the U.S. Navy. His bohemian attitude and blunt manner reminded her of the character Clark played. Within one month of their meeting, Bette startled everyone by marrying the recently discharged sailor. He was her third husband.

WEDDING OF ELEANOR POWELL AND GLENN FORD, 1943

❧

Bette Davis gave Glenn Ford his first big break in *A Stolen Life* (1946), but playing the part of Johnny Farrell in *Gilda,* that same year, made him a star. Ford's sexually ambiguous role meant slapping around the lead, Rita Hayworth, the new Hollywood sex goddess. Eleanor Powell, the tap-dancing star of the thirties and forties, retired from films during her sixteen-year marriage to Ford.

WEDDING OF LANA TURNER AND STEPHAN CRANE, JULY 17, 1942

Lana didn't know that Crane's divorce wasn't final when she married him in Las Vegas, a ceremony attended by Judy Garland. Lana became pregnant with her daughter, Cheryl, a few months later, and remarried Crane in June 1943. Cheryl was born in July.

WEDDING OF JOHN HODIAK AND ANNE BAXTER, 1946

Anne Baxter went to private schools in New York and, at the age of eleven, studied drama with Maria Ouspenskaya, the Russian character actress. Not only did Anne win the Oscar for *The Razor's Edge,* she was also nominated for *All About Eve* (1950). Hodiak, a former Chevrolet stock clerk, entered films during the war years, when leading men were scarce (he was 4-F because of high blood pressure). The couple divorced in 1953.

JOHN HODIAK, LANA TURNER

Marriage Is a Private Affair, 1944
DIRECTOR: ROBERT Z. LEONARD
COSTUME DESIGNER: IRENE

Lana's favorite director was "Pop" Leonard, who used Lana in every scene in this movie. The stars at MGM always requested the designer Adrian to create their costumes, but if they couldn't get him, the next best thing was the woman who took his place, Irene. Lana had twenty costumes, including this extraordinary wedding gown of satin and tulle that she wore for the ceremony and reception.

❧

Baby married Bogey wearing something old (Bogey told the press it was him, but it was an ID bracelet he gave her); something new (her suit of pale pink wool); something borrowed (a hankie from Mom); and something blue (a slip with her name embroidered on it). Bogey wore gray flannel and cried during the ceremony. The marriage lasted until Bogey's death on January 4, 1957.

LAUREN BACALL

✣

How to Marry a Millionaire, 1953

DIRECTOR: JEAN NEGULESCO
COSTUME DESIGNER: WILLIAM TRAVILLA

Three models share an apartment and expenses, each attempting to catch a rich husband. This film is the remake of *The Greeks Had a Word for Them* (1932), which was costumed by Coco Chanel. William Travilla was nominated for the Oscar for costume design for *Millionaire,* which starred Lauren Bacall, Betty Grable, and sex goddess Marilyn Monroe. Coco didn't receive the same recognition for *Greeks* because the academy did not recognize costume designers until 1948. Bacall has the film's best line: when asked about dating an older man, she says, "Look at Roosevelt . . . look at Churchill . . . look at that old fella, what's his name . . . in *The African Queen.*" Of course she's referring to her husband, Humphrey Bogart.

ENGAGEMENT PARTY OF ARLENE DAHL AND LEX BARKER, 1951

Always beautiful and always interested in glamour, Arlene became the 1946 "Rheingold Beer Girl" before going to Broadway and then on to Hollywood. In 1951, Arlene married Lex Barker, one of Hollywood's Tarzans (1949–1953), wearing a gown by Helen Rose. In the early eighties, Arlene appeared on TV's *One Life to Live,* and also became a syndicated beauty columnist.

WEDDING OF ARLENE DAHL AND FERNANDO LAMAS IN LAS VEGAS, 1954

What was Hollywood to do when Ricardo Montalban was busy? Use South American film star Fernando Lamas, who became one of the MGM "Latin Lovers" of the fifties. His marriage to Arlene Dahl lasted six years and their major production was Lorenzo Lamas, star of TV's *Falcon Crest.* When Fernando and Arlene got married in Vegas, they looked "maaaaahvelous."

WEDDING OF JUDY GARLAND AND VINCENTE MINNELLI (LOUIS B. MAYER, BEST MAN), JUNE 18, 1945

Judy Garland's boss, Mayer, was thrilled when she decided to marry MGM director Vincente Minnelli, who had directed her in the exquisite MGM musical *Meet Me in St. Louis* (1944). Judy had threatened to move to New York for a stage career, and this union seemed to ensure that she would stay in Hollywood. The wedding took place at Judy's mother's home in Los Angeles, Judy's dress, a smoky-gray jersey with pink pearl beading, was designed by MGM designer Irene. Baby Liza was born the following year.

WEDDING OF ALFRED STEELE AND JOAN CRAWFORD, 1956

This was not a typical Joan Crawford–planned production: Joan and her dinner date, Alfred Steele, jumped on his private plane to Vegas sans luggage, and said their vows in the penthouse of the Flamingo Hotel. Al, who was the board chairman of Pepsi-Cola, had to borrow a ring, and Joan had to borrow a nightie and a toothbrush. When Steele died three years later, Crawford became an active board member of Pepsi, also handling the publicity for the giant corporation.

WEDDING OF JOANNE WOODWARD AND PAUL NEWMAN, JANUARY 29, 1958

Just prior to their marriage, Paul and Joanne costarred for the first time in *The Long Hot Summer* (1958). They met in 1953 and got married at Hotel El Rancho Vegas in Las Vegas. They've had many collaborations, both on and off the screen. Paul's debut as a film-maker was directing Joanne in the Oscar-nominated film *Rachel, Rachel* (1968).

WEDDING OF FRANK SINATRA AND MIA FARROW, JULY 19, 1966

Frank and Mia got married at the home of Jack Entratter, Frank's good friend, who was the president of the Sands Hotel in Vegas. Red Skelton was a member of the bridal party, even though his wife had been accidentally shot the night before. Mia wore a white silk faille dress with rhinestone buttons, but her new pixie haircut got all the attention. After seeing a news photo of the wedding, one of Frank's former wives, Ava Gardner, said, "I always knew he'd end up in bed with a boy."

GEORGE LAZENBY, DIANA RIGG

✧

On Her Majesty's Secret Service, 1969

DIRECTOR: PETER R. HUNT

COSTUME DESIGNER: MARJORY CORNELIUS

And we thought James Bond and his only bride would live happily ever after. Diana Rigg, who was Emma Peel on TV's *The Avengers* series in the sixties, wore a white eyelet gown with an organdy overcoat. George Lazenby, in his first movie role, played Bond for the only time. The wedding couple's car was decorated with flowers to match the bride's dress, but, unfortunately, the bride and the marriage lasted only another few minutes. The flowers didn't survive, either.

CHARLES GRODIN, CYBILL SHEPHERD

⚜

The Heartbreak Kid, 1972
DIRECTOR: ELAINE MAY
COSTUME DESIGNER: ANTHEA SYLBERT

Lenny dumps his overweight Jewish bride on their honeymoon for a gorgeous blonde shiksa, played by Cybill Shepherd. Charles Grodin is Lenny, a shy newlywed with a mean streak, who first marries May's real-life daughter, Jeannie Berlin, in an informal Jewish wedding, and then marries WASP Cybill in a formal church wedding. Although director Elaine May wanted an actress with blond, flyaway hair to play the role of the second wife, the first actress cast had dark, coarse hair. Costume designer Anthea Sylbert took the young woman to a colorist and then to a specialist for texture-change treatments, but, after all that, she was replaced by Cybill Shepherd, a natural blonde. The unnatural one's hair fell out!

DENZEL WASHINGTON, ANGELA BASSETT

⚜

Malcolm X, 1992
DIRECTOR: SPIKE LEE
COSTUME DESIGNER: RUTH E. CARTER

In this film, Malcolm's maternal grandmother is raped by a white man, so his mother chose the darkest black man she could find and married him. Their wedding picture is shown in this Spike Lee film, which he directed and adapted from Alex Haley's book. When Malcolm X (Denzel) marries Betty Shabazz (Angela), designer Ruth E. Carter dressed Angela Bassett as a modestly dressed Muslim: her head and upper arms were completely covered. Ruth said that the off-white chiffon softened Angela's features. The style of the sixties was evident in Denzel's wedding attire, especially the suit lapels.

AND THEY LIVED
Happily Ever After

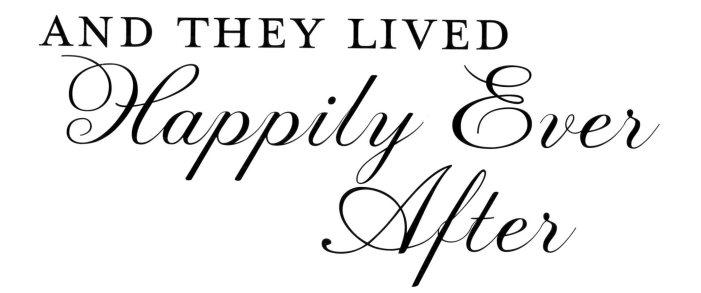

SPENCER TRACY, KATHARINE HEPBURN

Woman of the Year, 1942

DIRECTOR: GEORGE STEVENS
COSTUME DESIGNER: ADRIAN

Tess and Sam work for the same newspaper; he's the sportswriter, she's the political pundit who's been named "Woman of the Year." At first they hate each other, and then they fall in love and have a quick matrimonial moment—they're too busy for anything else. As Spence carries Kate into her apartment, the housekeeper says, "Good heavens, Miss Harding, have you been in an accident?" Although Tracy and Hepburn had a very long relationship, both on and off the screen, this scene never happened . . . except in the movies.